DECORATING WITH PLANTS

A HOUSE & GARDEN BOOK

DECORATING WITH PLANTS

Writer: Marybeth Little Weston

Editor: Barbara Plumb

Designer: Albert T. Hamowy

Pantheon Books · New York

Published in the United States by Pantheon Books, a division of Random House, Inc., New York, and simultaneously in Canada by Random House of Canada Limited, Toronto.

Library of Congress Cataloguing in Publication Data

Weston, Marybeth Little.
    Decorating with Plants.
    "A House & Garden book."
    1.   House plants in interior decoration.
I.   Title.
SB419.W25   747'.9   77-16138
ISBN 0-394-42680-0

Manufactured in the United States of America   First Edition

Contents

Acknowledgments

A book like this is naturally a potpourri of many talents. To the owners, architects, interior designers, and plant designers whose imagination and taste inspired this book, praise and thanks. Special thanks, too, to the editors who discovered and developed each story — Mary Jane Pool, editor-in-chief of *House & Garden*, and all her staff, with special nods to: Elizabeth Sverbeyeff Byron, Patricia Corbin, Miki Denhof, Jacqueline Gonnet, Margaret Kennedy, Joyce MacRae, Will Mehlhorn, Denise Otis, Kaaren Parker, Eleanor Phillips, Barbara Portsch, Babs Simpson, and Dorothea Walker. Special thanks also goes to Louis Oliver Gropp, editor-in-chief of the *House & Garden Guides*, and to the photographers who brought each room to life.

For botanical and editorial advice, thanks to T. H. Everett, James Fanning, Susan Sutton Handy, and to Donna Bass of Pantheon.

The spelling and standardization of botanical names is based on *Hortus Third*, by the staff of the L. H. Bailey Hortorium, Cornell University (New York: Macmillan Publishing Company, 1976). Pronunciation of genus names in the chart at the end of the book is based on a system devised by Ralph Bailey, garden editor of *House & Garden* (1954 – 1968).

Marybeth Little Weston
Garden Editor, *House & Garden*

Introduction

Plants have become so much a part of living today that we sometimes forget that decorating with house plants is a rather recent phenomenon. Early civilizations in temperate climates — parts of China, India, Egypt, Greece, Rome — left traces of enclosed courtyards with lily ponds and elegant earthenware flowerpots. But in northern climates, nature was often hostile. Plants were appreciated for food and shelter, and in brief bouquets, but in bitter cold winters, the only plants that leafed and bloomed appeared in paintings and tapestries. Even into our own century, house plants were a rarity, except for those grown in laboriously heated greenhouses.

Put your fingertips over the plants in the pictures in this book, and the rooms, though handsomely furnished, will suddenly seem bare. Lift them, let the plants flourish — and just see what decorating with a green thumb can do.

With today's large windows, innovative lighting, and heating-cooling systems that keep rooms comfortable winter and summer, we can grow a great range of plants. Indoor plants are more popular than ever before, and indoor gardeners are moving toward more creative ways of thinking about plants. Higgledy-piggledy collections are fading out; and the decorative potential of plants is just beginning to be explored.

With this book, perhaps you will look at your plants and rooms with new eyes, and imagine what you can do. Your own decorating style might be a factor in deciding what to grow. Some plants have an almost time-capsule connotation. With seventeenth- and eighteenth-century furniture, an orangerie of small citrus trees would be fitting, as would plants pruned to topiary forms. With Chippendale and Chinese Export porcelains, a plant with a Far East look, such as a fishtail palm or a polyscias, could be appropriate. For simpler eighteenth-century furnishings, you might consider herbs and potted paperwhites. Palms, ferns, and ivy have an authentic Victorian heritage, as do orchids that were pampered in glass-domed conservatories and geraniums that brightened farm and city window sills. Vines and lilies evoke the graceful, organic forms of Art Nouveau. Cyperus plants, with the look of Egyptian papyrus, suggest Art Deco, as does spathiphyllum with its flowers like calla lilies. The choice is at its widest with eclectic contemporary furnishings that seem compatible with plants from all over the world.

Knowing the history and geography of a plant can suggest sophisticated new combinations. As early as the seventeenth century, European explorers were bringing home exotic plants from the New World to delight their royal courts: for instance, the common inchplant, tradescantia, is named for Charles I's world-traveling gardener, John Tradescant, and his son. Eighteenth-century explorers in South Africa found the geranium; nineteenth-century travelers brought back chlorophytum and the African violet. Early visitors to China returned with aspidistra, gardenia, and chrysanthemums. Japan provided more chrysanthemums and the hydrangea. From equatorial Africa came dracaenas and sansevierias, and from the South Pacific, more dracaenas, many ferns, palms, orchids, cordylines, crotons, dizygotheca, and kangaroo ivy. Our own hemisphere, South America primarily, was the source of philodendrons, dieffenbachias, begonias, many orchids, and the bromeliads. Some of these plants were grown in nineteenth-century homes, despite gaslights and coal fires, but the widespread phenomenon of indoor gardening belongs to our own era.

In our practical man-made world, perhaps we are in special need of the living, breathing link with nature that plants provide. And because recent innovations in lighting, decorating, and architecture have made plant growing easier, there are glorious plants, whatever one's lifestyle or budget.

Plants are more than mere ornaments. As living things they have needs that must be fulfilled to keep them healthy. Choosing the right plants for the right places, caring for them with intelligence and love, is basic good sense, even thrift, but there is nothing amiss in appreciating a plant's decorative values and what it can do for a room. When a plant takes a useful, everyday part in decorating, both plant and room are enhanced.

In this book you will find over 200 plant varieties. You will learn their names and see how they have been used by talented architects and interior designers. You will see the work of many *House & Garden* editors and photographers. You will learn how to care for plants, how much light each plant needs, how often they need to be watered. You will also learn how to pronounce the necessary botanical names, which will add to your assurance in selecting and understanding your plants. Good indoor gardening comes with experience, but confidence and imagination can make a green thumb grow greener.

1
Accents

Decorating with plants
to add color to rooms,
interest to windows

Changing a room's color
with plants

Accenting paintings,
porcelain, sculpture,
drawings, prints

Using hanging baskets

Accenting ceilings,
floors, walls, fabric patterns,
and accessories with plants

Matching plants and
color schemes

Using plants as sculpture
or to enhance
the mood of a room.

Y̶ou have probably used plants as accents many times—for instance, moving a plant from a sunny window to a festive dinner table or to a guest's bedroom. When a plant can take a useful, everyday role in decorating, however, it gives a room a stepped-up vitality. A pale room can take on color; a sleek room, a more human scale. Plants furnish rooms without being ponderous, adding their own natural gleam.

Plants thrive with today's decorating, in rooms often white, with windows simply curtained, if at all, and in rooms with colorful lacquered walls that bounce and ricochet the light plants need to grow. Plants' decorative values—color, size, proportion, texture, pattern, translucence, density—make them ideal accents when thoughtfully used.

Decorate with plants to add color to rooms or to strengthen a color scheme. Most plants are green, a color compatible with all colors. Green in itself is many colors, from the first tendrils of spring to the deep shade of a tropical forest. Bright flowering plants can also pick up a color or a fabric pattern, as can the foliage plants—multicolored bromeliads, caladiums, crotons, and tradescantias—that nature seems to have dipped in paint pots.

Decorate with plants to increase interest in windows. They can be gardens, whatever the view beyond. Use plants to accent paintings, porcelain, sculpture, drawings, and prints. Plants can give art works a new spatial dimension, for they are art forms in themselves, bits of living sculpture.

Plants also lead the eye to ceilings, floors, or far corners—a wonderful way to stretch space. Plants work architecturally, contrasting vertical lines with horizontal, curving lines with angular. Plants are decorative in their own right and enhance everything you love. Grow them and know them, for they can add magic to your home.

GREEN PLUS WHITE

Green plants accent the green cushions and quilt in this room, a blizzard of white walls, white wicker, white cubes, and upholstered furniture. Even the floor of self-stick vinyl squares is snowy white—a perfect background for the twin Ficus retusa trees (Indian laurel). An Asparagus densiflorus (asparagus fern) and seasonal touches of potted-up Sedum spectabile, Queen-Anne's-lace, and Sinningia speciosa (gloxinias) repeat the pattern of an antique quilt. Interior designer: Gary Crain.

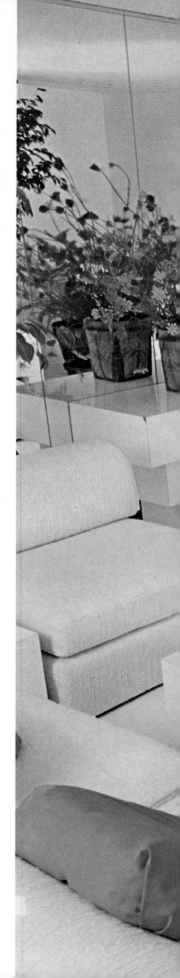

ERNST BEADLE

PLANTS FOR COLOR AT WINDOWS

Left: In this city apartment, sunlight filters through plants in windows and doors that open onto a narrow terrace greenhouse. A Ficus benjamina (weeping fig) in the left window; Nephrolepis exaltata 'Bostoniensis' (Boston fern), avocado, Citrofortunella mitis (Calamondin orange), and colorful Iresine Lindenii (bloodleaf) in the middle; plus a leathery Ficus lyrata (fiddle-leaf fig) at the right add color to this country-like room with taupe walls and American antiques. Lights accent plants at night. For George E. Schoellkopf by interior designers Harry M. Schule and Ned R. Marshall.

BULBS FOR SEASONAL ACCENTS

Right: Pure sunny color delivered in a plain brown wrapper—that's what a bulb is. Tulips, daffodils, hyacinths, and Muscari (grape hyacinths) staged on a window sill, coffee table, and country floor bring the color of spring indoors while leafless trees are still sheathed in ice. For added height, some of the pots are set on bricks. Bulbs are potted in September for Christmas, in early October for New Year's, in mid-October for Valentine's.

Tip: To force bulbs, use porous soil, set bulbs tip up, and cover with soil. Label and date them, water from top or bottom, then let drain. Next, store in a cool, dark place— 35°–48° F (2°–8° C)—for 12–15 weeks, and water occasionally. Take out of storage a month before desired bloom. Sprouts should be 1–3 inches high. Move to a warmer, semi-dark spot— 55°–60° F (13°–59°C) for 1–2 weeks. Water. Move to sunlight—65°–70° F (18°–21°C)—to bloom.

FLOWERING PLANTS FOR CHANGEABLE COLOR

In spring this indoor gardener fills her apartment hallway with yellow and orange tulips and greenhouse-grown calceolarias (pocketbook flowers) to make a golden garden. Some of the tulips are grouped around the trunk of a neatly pruned Ficus retusa.

In winter the hall is filled with white flowers, topiary chrysanthemums trained as standards, and cyclamens that cluster like butterflies around the base of the tree in its classic Versailles box. The glimmering Tiepolo frescoes, transferred to canvas, are 200 years old. Owner/designer: Enid Haupt.

Tip: Potted chrysanthemums, if kept well watered, will last a long time and may bloom again. Some can even be comfortably moved to your garden. To grow treelike standards, stake 12-inch cuttings. Prune off side shoots —sparing single leaves to produce chlorophyll —until tip grows to desired height. Then pinch it to encourage top branching.

12

FLOWERS WITH PAINTINGS AND PORCELAIN

Left: Decorating with plants takes on new meaning if you let a work of art inspire you. To complement the extraordinary pink in this Matisse, one collector experimented, found the perfect Pelargonium hortorum (geranium), and now propagates it for almost year-round use. Sometimes she uses cut blossoms with a collection of porcelain vegetables, with the result that colors and shapes seem to spill right out of the painting. Owner/designer: Enid Haupt.

PLANTS WITH A PAINTING AND PORCELAIN

Above: For a blue and white painting by Picasso, and Chinese ginger jars, here's another inspiration: a pair of multi-faced Hippeastrum (amaryllis), whose contrasting red blooms and yellow stamens, sculptural leaves and even shadows, accent the painting's colors and lines. Under the table, a low-light Cissus rhombifolia (grape ivy). Interior designer: Arthur Smith.

Tip: Amaryllis bulbs grow indoors in 8 weeks without a cooling period. They like to be tucked halfway into the earth in small pots whose diameters are only about 1½ inches wider than the bulb.

HORST P. HORST

FLOWERS WITH AN ART COLLECTION

Above: In this home gallery, all white and superbly track-lit, a basket of informal seasonal flowers — this time, Chrysanthemum frutescens (marguerites) — stands between paintings by Ron Cooper and Jim Dine. The sculptures, gold and black, are by Doug Edge. On the white floor, a Chinese rug suggests a cool lily pond. Interior designers: Mica Ertegün and Chessy Rayner of MAC II.

FLOWERS FOR COLOR WITH SCULPTURE

Right: Lean, angular Giacometti sculptures, combined with sunny flowers in earthy flowerpots, light up a stairwell in the apartment hallway of this collector. For the grouping, rounded flowers are always chosen — sometimes these plump calceolarias, or sometimes wax begonias — to add their counterpoint of shape and color. Owner/designer: Enid Haupt.

Tip: Flowers need sunlight or special lights to blossom, but the lighting used to accent art is enough to keep foliage plants thriving.

PLANTS TO COMPLEMENT COLOR IN ART

Above: In a city dining room that looks out on a sculpture garden, pots of pink Begonia semperflorens (wax begonias) and Hydrangea macrophylla (hydrangeas) link such tall foliage plants as Dieffenbachia maculata 'Jenmannii' (dumb cane) and a Monstera deliciosa (split-leaf philodendron). The sculpture is by Alexander Liberman; the painting is by Cleve Gray, as is the papier-mâché sculpture by the door. The ribbon-leaved plant is a Pandanus Veitchii (screw pine) Space-enhancing strips of mirror surround the window and door, and the right wall of the garden has a horizontal mirror to double the impact of plants and art. Owners/designers: the Alexander Libermans.

PLANTS WITH DRAWINGS AND SCULPTURE

Below: In the library, pots of white azaleas and white Primula obconica (German primrose) in season keep company with tropical plants: Ficus benjamina trees, a Dracaena cincta, and a Dracaena fragrans. The drawings are by Léger. Much of the sculpture is African. Window light here is supplemented by 100-watt floodlights attached to shelves, and the white, light-reflecting walls.

Tip: The secret of compact full-flowering begonias and geraniums is to pinch-pinch-pinch without remorse, to make each growing tip produce not one but many flowers.

NORMAN MCGRATH

ELLIOT ERWITT

PLANTS FOR COLOR ACCENTS OVERHEAD

Left: Three hanging plants on eye-hooks put greenery overhead and divide this large room into music, sleeping, and dining areas. They are grape ivy, Plectranthus australis (Swedish ivy), and Tradescantia albiflora (wandering Jew). Two Ficus benjamina trees, an elephant-eared Colocasia esculenta, and a Brassaia actinophylla (schefflera) are big enough to read or picnic under. Plant pedestal-cubes double as back rests. For Peter Link by architect Lee Pomeroy of Pomeroy-Lebduska Associates.

PLANTS TO ACCENT FLOOR COLOR

Above: In a skylighted city loft, a bower of plants accents the floor, painted an outdoorsy green and polyurethaned to be spillproof. Baskets of Chlorophytum comosum (spider plant), asparagus ferns, and Rhoicissus capensis (Cape grape) hang from chains secured to the beams. Like illusionary walls, other plants enclose living, work, and dining areas – a Ficus elastica (rubber plant), dieffenbachias, and avocados. Owners/artists: Roger Sandes and wife, Mary Welsh.

Tip: Hanging plants can be watered in various ways. Use a watering can and stepladder if the pots have attached saucers. Use an indoor hose if the floors are impervious. Or lift the plants off their supports once or more a week and water in a sink. Plants prefer lukewarm water.

GREEN TO ENLIVEN EARTH TONES

Left: American-Indian rugs and pillows, adobe vinyl floor, and brown leather furniture set a back-to-nature mood. Trees are a Ficus retusa and two young Ficus benjaminas. The pinkish bromeliad is a Neoregelia Carolinae 'Tricolor.' Interior designer: Doug Brinkman.

PLANTS TO EMPHASIZE A COLOR SCHEME

Above: For this subtle interplay of colors and forms in a dining room with mauve and blue batik, a pink abstract painting, and a lantern like a great white moon: a Caryota mitis (Burmese fishtail palm) and cratered-moon-like pink and mauve hydrangeas. For Steven Merrill by interior designer Michael Taylor.

Tip: Ficus trees are a varied family of tropical figs. Ficus retusa has a more compact head and broader oval leaves than the weeping Ficus benjamina. Both are more like northern trees than are their cousins, the fiddle-leaf fig and rubber plant.

ERNST BEADLE

Tip: Hydrangeas are wonderful to decorate with but hard to grow unless you have a greenhouse or a sheltered, preferably seaside garden. Gift plants in spring should be kept cool, watered frequently, and set outside in summer. Lime added to the soil makes the flowers pink; aluminum sulfate makes them blue.

PLANTS TO ACCENT PATTERN AND PORCELAIN

Above: It was marvelous mimicry to add potted white hydrangeas to this room — all blue and white and inspired by Victorian furniture and Chinese porcelain ginger jars, whose pattern is repeated in the fabric. White louvered shutters and white painted floors boost light, and slim lamps make the room inviting for reading. Interior designer: Joseph Braswell.

PLANTS TO ACCENT FABRIC AND WALLS

Right: Pink hydrangeas, a bouquet of roses and peonies, and a graceful fishtail palm seem to grow right out of the painted walls, complementing the flowery fabric. The wall was painted by an artist who copied an 18th-century English wallpaper to make this sitting room both a real and a make-believe garden. For the Warren Hopkins Clarks by interior designer Michael Taylor.

HORST P HORST

Tip: Boston ferns are an amiable and varied indoor plant. The many cultivars, including ruffled and lacy forms, need indirect light, even moisture, some misting, and the same kind of temperatures you find pleasant.

COLOR IN PLANTS TO ACCENT PRINTS

Above: Just one fern and one small bouquet make this room, with its fine botanical prints and leaf-green floral paper and fabric, a green retreat. The Boston fern and marigold bouquet repeat the colors of the prints, as do their natural containers. Interior designers: Mica Ertegün and Chessy Rayner of MAC II.

COLOR IN PLANTS TO ACCENT A PAINTING

Right: Pale floor, pale walls, and pale bed create a serene atmosphere in a room where a William Pettit painting above the bed has all the color. Miltonia orchids take their cue from the painting and intensify all the colors, including striped pillow cases and the green of the bedspread border.

GREEN WITH GENTLE COLORS

Left: Depending on the light, this room sometimes seems faintly pink, sometimes golden. It is painted a honey ivory and carpeted in wood-toned sisal, topped in the living room with shaggy goat-hide rugs. In contrast to the softness spiky Phormium tenax appear in the corners. For Marty and Gail Stayden by interior designer Jay Steffy.

GREEN WITH NATURALS

Above: Everything in this apartment shows an inventive use of naturals: wicker, wood, leather, stone, silver. The sitting room has a divider of slim alder trunks, stripped of their bark and sandblasted to form a see-through wall toward the kitchen. Near a decoupage by Silas Hathaway, a vriesea bromeliad in flower stretches past a leather screen toward Mineo Mizune's sculptured wood screws and a Cambodian silver melon. Interior designer: Michael Taylor.

Tip: Bromeliads are sturdy plants with an astonishing variety of forms. You can start a collection with the top of a pineapple bought at a grocery store. Scalp it, let top and leaves dry for a day, and set in soil. Water bromeliads in the vaselike whorl at top instead of drenching the soil.

PLANTS AS LIVING SCULPTURE

Below: Tall green verticals – an artful combination of angular, rounded, and spiky sculptural forms – add zing to a room of bold horizontal lines. The plants include a cactus-like Euphorbia canariensis, dieffenbachia, and yucca. Architect: Marcello d'Olivo. Interior designer: Paolo Permisi.

PLANTS AS MOOD ACCENTS

Above: The decorating in this apartment is a reminder that there are still new ways to use nature's gifts. The sofa is supple tobacco-brown leather, the dining chairs are reed, the lounge chair is wicker, the floor is travertine. Paired Strelitzia reginae (bird-of-paradise) are the dramatic accent, framing the skirted table and hurricane lamp. On the ledge behind, made of fossilized stone, are bromeliads. Interior designer: Michael Taylor.

Tip: A few dramatic specimen plants take less care than a variety of small ones. Watering needs are simplified. Some plants (like desert plants) drink a lot but seldom. Many tropicals drink a lot and often.

2
Living Spaces

Plants all through the house, and how they can make…

Living rooms more alive, more colorful, more comfortable

Dining rooms more inviting, roomier, like picnic spots

Kitchens more hospitable, personal, versatile

Bedrooms more serene, romantic, bright to wake up to, and restful to come home to

Bathrooms more playful, like water gardens or woodland pools

Hallways more welcoming, always in bloom

Plants all through the house

Any room people like, an unfinicky plant will like. (Finicky plants can be admired at botanical gardens, where experts can pamper them; we suspect that you're too busy.)

Living rooms, with their bright and softly lighted areas, are often convivial for plants. The thoughtful lighting, ventilation, and temperature conditions you plan for your guests and yourself will suit many plants.

Dining rooms decorated with plants become more inviting, like picnic spots. Here, floor space and traffic patterns often relegate plants to one wall or a buffet or a tabletop. Although spiny or sprawling plants are usually inconvenient, and sun-loving flowering plants are often ill-suited to the dining area, the range of low-light plants from which to choose is wide.

Like dining rooms, kitchens also become more personal, hospitable, and versatile when accented by plants. Because kitchens, too, often have narrow traffic lanes and limited floor and counter space, choose plants for your high shelves or window sills, and hang them from the ceiling — unless you are lucky enough to have a kitchen greenhouse. Herbs in a kitchen are handy.

Bedrooms with plants are nice to come home to but decide on just a carefree few. A tree that requires little floor space but spreads a leafy canopy is a good choice, but a huge, prickly cactus or a plant casting eerie shadows, such as a monstera, could be disturbing. If you keep a cool bedroom, here is an opportunity to enjoy ferns.

In a bathroom, a few plants reflected in a mirror can seem like many, and with the high humidity plants will flourish, particularly ferns, ivies, orchids, and many tropicals.

Hallways and stairways, if dark and narrow, are hazardous with floor-level plants. Today more and more hallways are lighter, wider, and hospitable to greenery.

Plants should be an asset, not a menace, to your decorating. A room with layers of curtains, wall-to-wall carpeting, and easily stained furniture and fabrics may be best with just one or two plants in special cachepots. If you're decorating with light-filtering shades, no-fuss floors, and treated spillproof fabrics, or if you think plants make any room more livable, use them all through the house.

ROOM FOR PLANTS AND PEOPLE

In this living room, with its lofty ceiling and window walls, are Cyperus Papyrus (paper plant) and Boston fern at the left; Ficus benjamina, chrysanthemums, Dracaena cincta, cereus, Alsophila Cooperi (tree fern), a small Crassula argentea (jade tree) and a Chlorophytum comosum 'Vittatum' (white-striped spider plant). Owner/architect: Jonathan B. Isleib of Interdesign.

JOHN T. HILL

LIVING ROOM SUNNIER
WITH PLANTS

When a young family remodeled a big old house (they even did the color-band painting together), out went curtains and in came sunshine and a parade of plants, some from the adjoining greenhouse: a shiny Asplenium nidus (bird's-nest fern), Polyscias Balfouriana, grape ivy, and Hedera Helix (English ivy). In spring, the family makes use of seasonal daffodil bulbs and forsythia branches. For the Aaron Lockers by interior designer: Joseph D'Orso.

Tip: The bird's-nest fern, a rosette of translucent leaves with a dark nest-like center, is a striking house plant for a spot with indirect light and good humidity. Start with a small one, which will more readily adapt to your house or apartment conditions.

34   ERNST BEADLE

TOM YEE

LIVING ROOM FOR ART AND PLANTS

Left: A single Ficus benjamina, a graceful sculpture in itself, takes its place with a sculpted torso and a painting by Kenneth Noland. The curve of the trunk repeats the curve of the figure as well as the woodiness of a twig construction by Charles Arnoldi. Track lighting accents art and plants. Primula obconica and Primula polyantha (primroses) are on a deck near a sliding glass door. Architect: Paul Gray of Warner and Gray.

LIVING ROOM WITH PLANTS FOR COLOR

Above: For a man who likes to work where he lives, an office/living room with a neutral color scheme is perked up by a red table, potted marigolds, and a few house plants for color: two Boston ferns, a Cussonia spicata, and two Pandanus Veitchii. The painting is by David Gibbs. Owner/designer: Lee Bailey.

Tip: Radiators under windows are a common problem, solved by perlite or pebble-filled trays painted to match the sill and elevated on wood blocks or a cork base. Fill trays with quarts of water every few days to keep soil moist and to make air humid for plants.

LIVING ROOM CHEERFUL WITH PLANTS

Left: An indoor tree that stays green all winter and pots of tulips brought into winter bloom add extra sparkle to a cheerful red room. The tree is a Ficus retusa. Furniture, fabrics, and wall covering by interior designer Billy Baldwin.

LIVING ROOM COOLED WITH PLANTS

Below: Woolly Hudson Bay blankets, sold by the yard for slip covers, prepare this room for a change of season. (The blankets have been famed since fur-trading days, when the number of black stripes at the corner told how many beaver skins the blanket was worth.) The plants are Ficus retusa, schefflera, Chrysalido-carpus lutescens (areca palm). Interior designer: Dan Hawkins.

Tip: Plants can't grow fur or ruffle their feathers to adjust to temperature or climate changes. They often adjust to heat by shedding leaves that transpire needed moisture. Most plants will leaf out again when they've adapted to your house temperature.

DAVID MASSEY

TOM YEE

LIVING ROOM BIG AS ALL OUTDOORS

*Left: The paneling in this living room came from country barns, and the cut
flowers and foliage plants provide an additional outdoorsy accent. Boston ferns
thrive at the foot of a weeping Ficus benjamina that will never have to worry
about bumping the ceiling. The sparkling white floors are tile and easy to clean.
Owners/designers: the Bruce Addisons. Interior designer: John Rieck.*

LIVING ROOM/LIBRARY WITH A TOUCH OF THE OUTDOORS

*Above: Starting with the colors in an 18th-century portrait of a young boy, the
colors of this room quickly fall into place: red walls, blue upholstery and
porcelains, and a geometric painting by Alexander Liberman. The red flowers
are Rieger begonias; the palms, Howea Forsterana (kentia palms).
Interior designer: Mario Buatta.*

**Tip: Feel the soil to judge
whether a plant needs water, or
use a matchstick to test the
depth of dryness.**

**Avoid set watering schedules,
as much depends on
temperature, humidity,
and whether the pot is of dry,
porous clay or teetotaling plastic.**

HORST P HORST

41

ERNST BEADLE

DINING ROOM WITH PLANTS THAT SAY WELCOME

Above: Oak chairs ring a modern Parsons table set with rabbit tureens, tree-trunk candlesticks, and bandana napkins, which pick up the red of geraniums along the window wall facing south. The old-brick floor is banked with geraniums, gardenias, grape ivy, Boston ferns, and a Ficus retusa. The beams are hung with Swedish ivy and a Zebrina pendula. Owners/designers: the Bruce Addisons. Interior designer: John Rieck.

DINING ROOM INVITING WITH PLANTS

Right: What was a basement storage room in an 1870 house has been glassed in, cobbled, and the stone walls stuccoed white. Natural wood chairs are pulled up to a long trestle table, and plants add to the sense of welcome: a hanging Philodendron lacerum over an asparagus fern, a young Dracaena fragrans 'Massangeana' near a Ficus benjamina 'Exotica,' farther back, a schefflera, and grape ivies hung on beams. Architects: Adolf deRoy Mark and Girvin W. Kurtz.

Tip: Hanging a plant from an exposed beam is easy with screw-in eye-hooks. If beams are concealed, tap to see if they are spaced at the usual 16-inch intervals from the corner. In doubt? Use a butterfly bolt, the only safe way with plasterboard.

42

TOM YEE

ELLIOT ERWITT

HORST P HORST

ERNST BEADLE

DINING ROOM WITH PLANTS ALOFT

Left, above: Two young artists live in a loft with plants as illusionary walls separating dining, living, and work areas. These include a hanging Cape grape, a chlorophytum, and an asparagus fern. Standing plants include a schefflera and a dieffenbachia. Owners/ artists: Roger Sandes and his wife, Mary Welsh.

DINING ROOM WITH TABLE PLANTS

Left, below: A young woman put old furniture to work by painting it white, then added a glass table. Her centerpiece is a tray of Saintpaulia ionantha (African violets). On the sideboard are Swedish ivy, Boston fern, English ivy, Nerine (an amaryllis relative), Spathiphyllum 'Clevelandii,' and Aechmea fasciata (urn plant). Interior designer: William Hodgins.

DINING ROOM WITH A SUNSHINE MOOD

Above: With paint and rugs like sunshine, two mirrors and lots of wicker, this dining room, with a 13-foot dark refectory table, has a sunny spirit. One of the three Boston ferns is raised on a small wicker table, because the owner prefers out-of-the-way end pieces to centerpieces. Nearby, a column of Cape grape and cut chrysanthemums repeat colors. Owner/designer: Van day Truex.

Tip: African violets and spathiphyllum are among the few plants that bloom profusely throughout the year without direct sunlight. Violets can be fussy, but spathiphyllum is a die-hard.

TOM YEE

DINING ROOM WITH COUNTRY FLOWERS

Left: When sun streams in through south windows, geraniums can bloom as beautifully indoors as out. For this dark-beamed country dining room, with red cushions, curtains, and a bold durrie rug, what could be better? Interior designers: Keith Irvine and Thomas Fleming.

DINING ROOM WITH SHADE PLANTS

Above: For this room with light-reflecting red lacquered walls, a round table, and a paper lantern, plants are plentiful and set around well out of the traffic flow. Shade-tolerant Impatiens Wallerana blooms on the buffet, while an artfully pruned Ficus benjamina and a white browallia catch some light at the window. Some plants get by under the Parsons table. The painting above it is by Alexander Liberman: the silk-screen above the buffet is by I. Bolotowsky. Interior designer: Pamela Barker.

Tip: With plant care, don't hesitate to try some under-the-table tricks. Low-light plants don't mind airy hideaways. A foil underlining for a table could also disperse light as shiny lacquered walls do.

DINING IN A PICNIC MOOD

Above: With a parasol concealing a light fixture, a hanging basket of Tripogandra multiflora (fern-leaf inch plant), and a wicker plant cart holding chrysanthemums and Boston ferns, this is an inviting kitchen/dining area for two or for a crowd. Garden baskets hang on the wall within handy reach. Light floods the room except when matchstick shades are lowered. Owner/designer: Ray Kohn.

DINING UNDER AN INDOOR TREE

Right: To create the airiness of spring, the walls of a brick porch were painted white, the cement floor painted to resemble stone, and suddenly . . . an imaginative dining area. A bough of Ficus benjamina almost touching a basket of Philodendron scandens oxycardium (parlor ivy) makes a green canopy. Again matchstick curtains are used, providing adjustable light for geraniums and Polypodium aureum arecolatum. Interior designer: Richard Lowell Neas. Trompe l' oeil floor by Luis Molina.

Tip: A simple dining cart laden with small plants can give you a garden on wheels, handy for rolling to a light source and imbuing a collection of small plants with decorative importance.

KITCHEN MADE FOR HOSPITALITY

A jumble of five tiny rooms became one big kitchen for a family that loves to cook. The children especially enjoy bringing friends home to their soda fountain and popcorn wagon. Plants are up and out of the way but aren't the sort to sulk if not in the limelight. Grape ivy is happy above the cabinets but also grows in brighter light above the flower-fixing sink with its extra-high faucet. The primroses on the table are Primula polyantha. Architect: Peter Rooke-Ley. Interior designers: Ann Rooke-Ley and Maria Quinn.

Tip: Grape ivy makes a good member of the family. Fast-growing and beautiful, it is virtually pest-free. It is also easy to propagate from a friend's cuttings, and just one plant can make many in a short time. Because it is happy in sun or in a dim corner, it provides carefree greenery with no fuss.

DAVID MASSEY

TOM YEE

KITCHEN MADE PERSONAL WITH PLANTS

Above: An old, dark kitchen was remodeled with white stucco and tiles; the ceiling was lowered with beams at an angle; and green was used as the accent: two Ficus retusas, ferns, palms, ivies, and chrysanthemums. Above the table, palm fronds fill a bark basket. Interior designer: Louis Bromante.

KITCHEN MADE PERSONAL WITH HERBS

Right: This is the kitchen of a good cook who likes to garden. In an 18th-century forge, converted into a family retreat, herbs grow on a window sill, alongside an African violet. Herbs from outdoors, along with an achimenes, hang from a beam. Owners/designers: John F. and Virginia Saladino.

Tip: If you spend much time in the kitchen, why not let plants keep you company? This way you won't forget to water and bathe them (plants like a mild sudsy bath; pests do not), and they'll love the attention and humidity.

ERNST BEADLE

Tip: Fatshedera Lizei is a funny name but a dandy plant, the crossing of unlikely parents. Fatsia japonica is a shrub; hedera is an ivy. Their offspring is plump like the fatsias and has ivy leaves like the hederas. Give it lots to drink.

KITCHEN LIKE A GAZEBO

Below: In a small seaside cottage, hanging plants – two Swedish ivies, a grape ivy, lilies, and white petunias – plus trellised panels over a door and a small window, give this tiny kitchen the charm of a gazebo. Shadowy white wallpaper and white vinyl flooring suggestive of the brick courtyard beyond emphasize the summerhouse idea. Interior designers: Todd Stevenson and Peter Trani.

KITCHEN LIKE A GREENHOUSE

Right: Two pantries became a kitchen when this 1910 house was remodeled. The windows above the sink's splash panel stretch into the greenhouse roof above it. Some plants on the cabinets are begonias and Fatsia japonica, asparagus fern, Rieger begonias, and Fatshedera Lizei (tree ivy). Architects: Henry S. Reeder, Jr., and Joseph Maybank of Architectural Resources.

ERNST BEADLE

TOM YEE

KITCHEN WITH A CEILING FOR HANGING PLANTS

Streamlined but not a bit institutional, this is an efficient kitchen from floor to ceiling. Different shades of terra-cotta tile make spots no problem. Fluorescent tubes under wall-hung cabinets light the counters and make herb growing practical. The grid-frame ceiling is ideal for hanging baskets: asparagus fern, Pelargonium peltatum (ivy geranium), impatiens, grape ivy, and Boston fern. With the addition of a red-flowered tablecloth, the kitchen's mood swings from efficiency to festivity. Interior designer: Charles Mount.

Tip: Asparagus densiflorus 'Sprengeri' and other asparagus ferns are neither asparagus nor ferns. Their care resembles that of ferns but is easier — they don't need as much moisture in the air. However, what they do like is a good soaking in a bathtub or kitchen sink.

DUANE MICHAELS

KITCHEN WITH A LIVE-IN GREENHOUSE

Left: In this multipurpose kitchen for cooking, dining, laundry, sewing, and gardening, one wall is a standard lean-to greenhouse where orchids, begonias, palms, a Coffea arabica (Arabian coffee tree) and chrysanthemums thrive. A cabinet under the botanical poster is devoted to green-thumb needs. A Beloperone guttata (shrimp plant) is on the table.

KITCHEN WITH LIVE-IN HERBS

Above: All it takes to grow sun-loving plants, even herbs indoors year-round, is the endless summer of fluorescent light. Parsley, dill, chives, basil, sorrel, and an ornamental pepper plant grow in a tray filled with pebbles under two 24-inch warm-white and cool-white tubes. Herb tray is by Peter H. Dunlop.

Tip: Fluorescent lights for plants need not be purple-pink. Plants grow just as well under white light. Fluorescents require no more electricity than incandescent bulbs, give three times as much light for the wattage, and last longer.

BEDROOM BARE ESSENTIALS PLAYFUL WITH PLANTS

The bed is a bare fourposter; the tiled floor and sunny deck are barer still. Yet this iconoclastic bedroom has the charm of surprise. Its plants — Podocarpus macrophyllus (Southern yew), asparagus fern, and nubbly Schlumbergera Bridgesii (Christmas cactus) — repeat the texture of the bedspread with its tufts and tassels. Add the patchwork pillow cases and birdcage, and the harmony of texture and the humor are apparent. Owner/architect: Myron Goldfinger.

Tip: A plant's bare essentials are something to grow in, the right light, a temperature it prefers, the water it needs, food when it wants it, and some moisture in the air. Each plant is an individual, like each child in a family, but if you like the plants you grow and keep trying, plant parenthood can be fun.

PIER GIORGIO SCLARANDIS

BEDROOM LIKE A SUMMER PAVILION

Left: A blue canopy suggestive of blue sky, and a green Ficus benjamina, seem to mingle with the leafy world outside the window, transforming this bedroom with a fourposter into a holiday in the country. And wouldn't a noontime nap be nice? Interior designer: Manfred Ibel.

BEDROOM SERENE AS A SUMMER'S DAY

Above: Looking like the first day of summer, this bedroom/sitting room with sheet slipcovers is a place for good talk, good books, and leisurely unwinding, made private by the matchstick shades at the French doors. The Ficus retusa alongside the angled bed has a sheltering stance, while a Pityrogramma (silver fern) adds balance. Interior designer: Angelo Donghia.

Tip: Variety is the spice of life. Nature always lowers temperatures at night, and plants expect it. They need the drop both to absorb the sugars their leaves have made all day and to rest.

ERNST BEADLE

BEDROOM LIKE AN OASIS

Left: This is a private kingdom: a white room with a desert-beige carpet, a vibrant Soumak rug on the platform bed. Plants, baskets, and rocks are the only accessories. The color drawing is by Sol Lewitt. The cactus-like plant is a Euphorbia Milii (crown-of-thorns). Architect: Charles Marks.

BEDROOM WITH A TRELLIS AND A TREE

Above: For this room, sandy-pale like a long, smooth stretch of seashore, flecked with brown and blue pillows and backed by a bleached oak grille, a fishtail palm seems almost windblown. Interior designer: John F. Saladino, Inc.

Tip: Plants benefit from being neatly groomed. Remove and discard yellowing leaves and faded flowers. Snip off brown tips of leaves with manicure scissors. Loosen top soil of large plants once a year or replenish with a fresh layer.

HANS NAMUTH

BEDROOM BRIGHT TO WAKE UP TO

Left: Blue and white checked sheets and patchwork accessories in a white room needed only a touch of orangey-red to bounce to life. The plant is a Clivia miniata (Kaffir lily). Cut dogwood branches yawn and stretch at left. Roman shades regulate the light.

BEDROOM RESTFUL TO COME HOME TO

Above: A bedroom with a plant room to putter around in — what could be more relaxing? In this 1910 house, the plant room had been a screened-in sleeping porch. Shade-loving impatiens and other plants now grow there. Nearby are Boston ferns and a Dracaena cincta. Owner/architect: Jacquelin Robertson.

Tip: Plants outgrow pots as babies outgrow bassinets. When repotting, do it gently in a pot one size larger, tucking in the soil mixture firmly. The plant should not receive bright sun for a few days while it adjusts to the change.

ERNST BEADLE

PATTERNED BEDROOM STILLED WITH GREEN

Left: A slim-leaved Ficus benjamina and a gloxinia in flower add green serenity to a sophisticated interplay of matching geometrics. The patterns are in surprising melon, red, and blue, and were inspired, as was the paper, by the Bakuba culture of the Congo. They're complemented by wicker, basket trunks, and matchstick shades.

BEDROOM WITH THE FEELING OF SUNRISE

Above: Clearly, a nature lover lives here, with the sunrise colors for walls and quilt, hemp matting underfoot, and collections of plants, minerals, butterflies, geodes, shells, books, and baskets. Eucomis comosa (pineapple flower) and an aechmea are at the side. A Ficus benjamina stands in for curtains, and a vase holds cut zinnias and Gloriosa daisies. Room and modular fiberglass furniture by Marc Held.

Tip: One good turn deserves another. To keep plants from reaching toward the sun and growing lopsided, turn a pot a quarter-way or halfway around every week or two. For heavy plants, try a platform on wheels or casters, or a lazy Susan.

ERNST BEADLE

BEDROOM ROMANTIC AS MOONLIGHT

Left: This room has a dreamlike quality with its shadowy taupe walls, soft comforter and rug, and trailing heart-shaped leaves of Philodendron scandens oxycardium that garland the gleaming brass bed. The ceiling is painted with concentric circles of soft colors. For Marty and Gail Stayden by interior designer Jay Steffy.

BEDROOM LIKE A MORNING-GLORY

Above: In this 1738 farmhouse bedroom, the walls are bright as an arbor of blue morning-glories above a crocheted afghan and a sunny fabric scattered with leaves and flowers. The window sills are leafy with angel-wing begonias, Tolmiea Menziesii (piggyback plant), Philodendron scandens oxycardium, and at right, a chlorophytum catching the sun. Interior designer: Gary Crain.

Tip: To keep smooth leaves dust-free, wipe with a paper towel dipped in tepid water. For downy leaves like those of piggybacks and African violets, use an infant's hairbrush.

TOM YEE

Tip: Pedestals make small plants seem tall, bring them closer to the light, lift them off floors that are not spillproof, and move them beyond the reach of toddlers and pets. In a grouping of small plants, even an up-ended flowerpot can add height.

MULTIPURPOSE BEDROOM WITH PLANTS AS CURTAINS

Above: Plants seem twice as tall when they're staged on steps, pedestals, or swinging with no visible means of support. Because this bedroom is also a living room, the steps double as chairs, tables, and shelves, and give height to plants. The trees are Ficus benjamina and cassia. Smaller plants include a Sedum griseum, hanging Polypodium scolopendria fern and Ananas comosus (pineapple). Interior designer: Ann Bolitski.

BEDROOM BRIGHT WITH FLOWERING PLANTS

Right: Imagine waking up in this room just as the sun vaults over the horizon. With arched plexiglass windows at the gables, Cissus antarctica (kangaroo vine) and flowers like Rieger begonias get just the right light to prosper. Here the plant pedestal is a wicker hamper. Architect: Edward M. Coplon.

BATHROOM AS A WATER GARDEN

A fantasy, perhaps, but with prophetic ideas to inspire. An extra-deep tub is set in real grass in a pavilion near a pool. The water plants are tall Cyperus alternifolius (umbrella plant) and smaller varieties, erect-leaved Thalia dealbata, small-leaved Eichornia crassipes (water hyacinth),and Nymphaea (water lilies). The orchids are white cattleyas and greenish Paphiopedilum (lady-slipper). A fixed, slanted skylight is screened with a bamboo roller blind. Interior designers: William Machado and Norman Diekman.

Tip: Plants that live in water are a happy choice for people who travel, who forget to water, or whose generosity leaves other kinds of plants swimming. Just a soufflé dish with water and some pebbles can support a graceful cyperus. Give it good light and occasional soluble plant food.

BATHROOM AS A JUNGLE POOL

Left: High loft ceilings, exposed pipes, and plank floors show that this is an old building. A new tub of redwood and stainless steel was added and screened with plants: a palm, a small Dracaena fragrans, tall Polyscias Balfoureana, Grevillea robusta (silky oak), Licuala grandis (small fan palm), another dracaena and polyscias, and a spathiphyllum. Owner/artist: Alexandre Wakhevitch.

BATHROOM RENEWED WITH PLANTS AND PATTERN

Above: An old-fashioned tub in a once cheerless attic room is renewed with flowery sheets on walls and windows, a pink ceiling and sunny carpet, wicker, and plants. These include round-leaved Coccoloba Uvifera (sea grape), Polypodium aureum (hare's-foot fern), and in season, fragrant hyacinths. Interior designer: Gary Crain.

Tip: A pot, like a tub, must always be left clean. Before reusing a clay or plastic pot, scrub well in a solution of one part chlorine bleach to nine parts hot water. Rinse.

BATHROOM AS A SCULPTURE GARDEN

Left: This room was added to an older house as a narrow wing. Outside, a curved brick wall encloses a stone fountain. Inside, just a few plants are silhouetted against the wall and window, and are reflected in the mirror. The tall plant is a Codiaeum variegatum (croton) with asparagus ferns at its base. The twin pots hold Primula polyantha. Architect: W. Irving Phillips.

BATHROOM AS A FLOWER GARDEN

Above: A painted branch on a pink screen seems to take off from the tree geranium alongside it. Pots of Rieger begonias and white and red impatiens are dotted near a marvelous red tub, which could tempt a bather as a red flower tempts a hummingbird. Interior designer: Albert Hadley of Parish-Hadley.

Tip: A bathroom is a good place to grow ivy and other plants in colorful bottles filled with water. Keep water pure with a piece of charcoal from the fireplace, not the treated kind for barbecue grills.

ERNST BEADLE

Tip: Humor is not amiss in decorating with plants: kangaroo vine in an exercise room; baby's-tears in a nursery; thyme by a kitchen timer; a gift plant in a guest room for a friend named Rose, Rosemary, Daisy, or Basil.

BATHROOM LIKE A WOODLAND POOL

Above: Besides catching the reflection of a private woodland beyond sliding glass doors, this step-down tub is edged with ferns: two Boston ferns and a Polypodium subauriculatum (jointed fern) on a chain above. Even cymbidium orchids feel at home in this setting of rock, wicker, and earth-brown tile. Owner/designer: Manfred Ibel.

BATHROOM PLAYFUL WITH PLANTS

Right: In this bathroom that is also a stay-slim-with-exercise home gymnasium with rings and tufted mat, the plants are in keeping: kangaroo vine and Euphorbia Tirucalli (pencil tree). They're near a deep-soak tub between a shower and a restful stretch tub. Interior designer: John F. Saladino, Inc.

TOM YEE

**Tip: Greenhouse-grown plants
make guests welcome,
and also fit in as guests among
house- grown plants.
They will last a long time if
kept cool and out of direct light.**

HALLWAY INVITING WITH PLANTS

*Above: Theirs is a house that blooms indoors, starting with plants
in a glass-walled gallery that change with the seasons. These are
cascading chrysanthemums on pedestal frames. A Citrus sinensis
(sweet orange tree) grows in a big tub all year round, with ample
light from the sliding glass doors. For Governor and Mrs. Pierre
S. du Pont IV by architect I. W. Colburn.*

STAIRWAY ALWAYS IN BLOOM

*Right: Flowers and sunshine light up this Louis XVI curving
staircase. The flowers of the moment are calceolarias; sometimes
they are geraniums or wax begonias. The pots' saucers are earth-
colored plastic and moisture-proof. Owner/designer: Enid Haupt.*

Tip: To support tree-form plants or climbers that must be tied to stakes, use strips of nylon pantyhose cut as rings to rubber-band size. Almost invisible, they stretch with the growing plants.

SKYLIGHTED PASSAGEWAY WITH PLANTS

Below: When two separate buildings — parts of an old inn — were joined by glass walls, a skylight, and a paving of hexagonal tiles, the owners had a cozy house for themselves and an ideal place for such plants as citrus trees (orange and lemon), a hanging ivy geranium, a tree geranium, Dracaena deremensis 'Warneckii,' and Passiflora (passionflower) on a stake. For John and Tina Barney by architects John Smyth and Robert Liebreich. Interior design by Keith Irvine and Thomas Fleming.

SKYLIGHTED HALLWAY WITH PLANTS

Right: Two sections of a cottage, one old and one new, were sheathed with cedar siding and linked by a skylighted hallway paved with slate. Plants thrive here: a kangaroo vine, a Tripogandra multiflora, an oxalis in flower, and below them, a Swedish ivy. Owner/designer: Charles Mount.

3 Plant Rooms

LIVING IN A GREENHOUSE

Glassed to be open to sunlight and moonlight, and half tucked into a protective sandy berm anchored with grass, this house is designed to be at home with nature. An enormous panel, "Marilyn," by Andy Warhol, beckons visitors into the bold yellow entrance tunnel. Architects: Klein, Cohen, Klein.

BERNARD ASKIENAZY

Rooms made for plants

Greenhouses you live in, swim in, party in

Porches and terraces renewed with glass, latticework, greenery

Breezeways, galleries, halls, all spillproof

Bubble skylights, slanting skylights, electric lights

Your year-round garden

Agarden room is a state of mind. Any room where plants grow can be a garden room, but a room especially designed for plants, a room where people are often the temporary guests, is often the most innovative and magical in the house. More rooms, and even entire houses, are being planned today with the well-being of plants in mind: glass walls and roofs, greenhouse kitchens and hallways, rooms with skylights and special lights that let you switch on the sunshine. Some rooms even have built-in faucets and drains, and open-to-the-earth planting spaces.

But you don't have to build a house to have a plant room. Seldom-used porches, breezeways, upstairs sleeping porches, and rooftops can often be remodeled and put to year-round use. Attics can be opened with skylights; terraces can be enclosed; and standard greenhouse sections can be added, even to townhouses. Ordinary rooms can take on a new look with the addition of trelliswork, old furniture painted white, shelving, and plant lights. Modern technology has opened up all sorts of ways to combine the dwelling places of plants and people. In a plant room, you can feel you are outdoors even when you're indoors. You can garden all year round and enjoy your own private weather.

BERNARD ASKIENAZY

LIVE-IN GREENHOUSE, BY DAY

Viewed from the side in the daytime, the greenhouse in a sand dune becomes not at all futuristic but an integral part of a beach house. Ivy geraniums and grape ivy hang from the ceiling, and asparagus ferns sit on the counter. Adjustable metal blinds regulate the light, which is enough to filter down to the tiled hallway and a Cordyline australis and a young Philodendron Selloum. Architects: Klein, Cohen, Klein.

GREENHOUSE FARMHOUSE

In profile this contemporary house resembles a giant space station on a gloriously new planet. Actually it is a farmhouse combining spare efficiency and country space. At its core is a greenhouse, with a tropical half facing south and a temperate half facing north. Cast-stone awnings on the south side help keep rooms cool, and each room has its own deck area. A flying bridge connects rooms at each end. Architect: Paul Rudolph.

Tip: Catch all the sunlight you can, wherever you live. If a room is dark, paint it white. Keep windows sparkling clean. Wash off plant leaves so city grime or country dust can't screen out light. Use mirrors or aluminized plastic mirrors to bounce light from walls to plants.

TOM YEE

GREENHOUSE FARMHOUSE: THE LEAFY CORE

The greenhouse at the heart of this house encloses hallway and stairs. A flying bridge is edged by a barely noticeable sheet of plexiglass near an enormous English ivy. The bridge links the living/kitchen area (painting by Alice Forman) and a study/guest room wing. A floating staircase leads to and from the master bedroom. The tropical part of the greenhouse grows such plants as Cycas revoluta (sago palm) and Bougainvillea Buttiana, and below them, bromeliads, figs, nectarines, bananas, and orchids. Some are planted in an unpaved floor. In the cooler north-facing part of the greenhouse, azaleas, begonias, and ferns thrive. Some plants are rotated during the year for their own needs and for interesting color and textural combinations. The owners have also had success with tomatoes and peppers. Architect: Paul Rudolph.

Tip: You can grow tropical bougainvillea in just a sunny south window. Colorful bracts, like translucent tissue paper, appear several times a year if the air is kept humid.

SWIM-IN GREENHOUSE AND CABIN

A small house and a complete garden and swimming pool under glass were the dream of these indoor gardeners. They live in the north and figure their every-day's-a-holiday environment costs yearly only what a brief annual holiday in the tropics would. They bought and moved a 1927 estate greenhouse, 35 by 83 feet. Fin radiators provide heat, never below 60°F (15°C). The pool, heated separately, also provides warmth and humidity. Ordinary indoor plants, growing in the ground but with house-plant soil added to the planting holes, have gone wild here. Vines cover the structural poles. The tree over the pool is a Ficus benjamina 'Exotica.' Owners/designers: Roger Wohrle and Dick Waite.

ERNST BEADLE

Tip: Everyone can have fun with a miniature greenhouse for rooting cuttings quickly. Fill a see-through sweater box with 1½ inches of moist vermiculite, and tamp in 3-inch cuttings clipped below a leaf node. Replace lid for high humidity and keep out of direct sun.

94

LIVING-ROOM GREENHOUSE

Left: A derelict 90-foot greenhouse, vintage 1910, which came with a carriage house as an unsolicited bonus, was turned into a shaded, fan-cooled summer living room. Part of the greenhouse was left unglazed for use as a rose garden. Plants are a maranta (prayer plant), ficus, angel-wing begonia, rose tree, Nerium Oleander (oleander), areca palm, Boston fern, and ivy geraniums. Gloxinias brighten the table. Interior designer: Joan Peck.

DINING-ROOM GREENHOUSE

Above: In this white-tiled room with a ceiling like a giant glass umbrella, the red flowers are anthuriums, the reddish leaves, a variety of Cordyline terminalis (ti). The rest is lushly green: paired Ficus benjaminas, Boston ferns, striped Bromelia serra, pale Dieffenbachia maculata 'Rudolph Roehrs,' and farther in, a giant Philodendron Selloum, a Phoenix canariensis (date palm), hanging heart-leaved Philodendron scandens, and chlorophytum. Interior designer: John Wright.

Tip: If bare soil under an indoor tree bothers you or entices pets or toddlers to dig and scatter, cover it with dark polished river rocks or fir-bark chips, or underplant tree with a trailing plant.

ROBERT LAUTMAN

TERRACE GARDEN ROOM

Above: This porch, furnished like a garden, replaced an outside terrace. Gray plexiglass panels cut the glare; the floor is practical slate. Chrysanthemums, Senecio cruentus (cinerarias), and Solanum Pseudocapsicum (Jerusalem cherry) grow with an areca palm and Ficus retusa. For the Edward Burlings, Jr., by architect Hugh Newell Jacobsen. Interior designer: Luis Fernando Moro.

BREEZEWAY GARDEN ROOM

Right: An open walkway between garage and house became a plant room when the ends were enclosed and bubble skylights added. The room is air-cooled in summer, and a gas heater supplements house heat in winter. Waterproof gypsum board and exterior paint, used inside, are unfazed by moisture from a portable humidifier and even a wand hose. Uncommon plants thrive: Platycerium bifurcatum (staghorn fern), Philodendron 'Barryi,' caladium, aeschynanthus, passionflower, Pteris cretica, and oncidium and other orchids. For The A. Vandiveer Straits by Honey Mulligan Strait of Indoor Greenery.

Tip: If you're building or remodeling, discuss plants with your architect, contractor, and decorator. Installing ceiling lights or power and water outlets is easier, earlier.

TOM YEE

TRELLISED BACK PORCH

Left: Stretched across the rear of the house, this garden room is screened and latticed. It is roofed with plexiglass. When the sun is hot, the plexiglass is shaded with bamboo matting. The sofa is faced with extra trellis strips. Nested tables double as plant pedestals, and one holds a rex begonia. Some of the other plants include caladiums, crotons, geraniums, oleanders, Boston ferns, and chrysanthemums. Interior designers: Carmine Schiavone and Gerard Rebouillat.

TRELLISED SECOND-STORY PORCH

Above: This gazebo-like porch room has Philodendron cordatum climbing up its corner trellises, and reading lamps used as plant lights. Miltonia orchids in blue planters pick up the colors of the Kilim rug. On the table are paphiopedilum orchids.

Tip: In rooms where pets or children might be tempted to nibble leaves, it's wise to skip or postpone such toxic plants as oleander, Jerusalem cherry, philodendrons, caladium, or speech-paralyzing dieffenbachias (that's why they're called dumb cane).

TOM YEE

ROOFTOP PLANT ROOM

Left: Greenery in the midst of a city is doubly welcome. Here, below a Romanesque church dome, a glassed-in area paneled with mirrors boosts humidity for hanging grape ivy, lacy verbena, huge bird's-nest ferns, amaryllis, gloxinia, prostrate rosemary, tulips, and two kinds of narcissus, paperwhites and yellow 'Soleil d'or.' Owner/designer: Renée Graubart.

TOWNHOUSE PLANT ROOM

Above: A greenhouse in the rear courtyard of a townhouse enlarges an adjoining sitting room/dining room and is paved with matching tiles. On cloudy days, fluorescent tubes above plants and potting bench boost light for begonias, orchids, dracaenas, ferns, geraniums, wax begonias, and a camellia. Owner/ architect: Albert Swanke. Owner/designer: Pratt Swanke.

Tip: Fluorescent lights have the color spectrum seeds and flowers need. Incandescents with 150- and 200-watt lamps maintain low-light foliage plants and can be used 8–12 hours at distances of 3–6 feet. A 75-watt can be placed a little closer and used to uplight plants at night.

103

OVER-THE-GARAGE GREENHOUSE

Left: The only place to put a greenhouse here was right over the garage, and it worked. Gray glass, resembling metal when viewed from the street, is set between teak rafters. A sink at one end and potting benches on two sides surround a Ficus benjamina and a miniature orchard of citrus trees, plus geraniums and a dieffenbachia. Except for a monstera in the corner and an aeschynanthus, the work areas are mainly for orchids: dendrobium, oncidium, and phalaenopsis (moth orchid near the sink). For the Robert Eichholzes by architect Hugh Newell Jacobsen.

SKYLIGHTED GARDEN INDOORS

Right: Inside you think you might be outside. Tall trees knee-high in ferns grow in an open-to-the-earth bed in a skylighted living room/music room. The black dot in the skylight is one of several canister lights that stand in for sunshine at night. The trouble-free bed, left open when the house was built, is framed by waterproof slate. The tree is a Ficus benjamina 'Exotica,' with Boston ferns. The painting is by Gabor Petterdi. Architect: Hugh Newell Jacobsen.

Tip: Growing orange, lemon, and lime trees indoors is rewarding. You can even make marmalade. Essential for citrus trees are sun, acid soil (add extra peat and acid fertilizer), tepid water, and sometimes when they look pale, chelated iron. Keep cool.

ROBERT LAUTMAN

SKYLIGHTED HALL FOR PLANTS AND ART

Above: A cedar-beamed gallery, stretching across the whole front of the house, is the first room you enter. With its skylights and white walls and carpets, it dances with light even on gray days. The gallery houses the beginnings of a plant collection: a Chamaedorea erumpens (bamboo palm) and Cordyline australis. For the John Gaineses by architect Barry V. Downs.

SKYLIGHTED HOUSE FOR PLANTS AND VIEWS

Right: Oriented to the south and with almost every wall glassed to catch a view, this house is filled with light, and plants grow in every room. These are a kentia palm, Boston fern, and Ficus retusa. Owner/architect: Rodney Friedman.

Tip: Recently purchased plants are, or should be, in good soil to serve their needs. Points to check: Is soil loose enough to admit water and air to the roots? Is it too porous, letting water run through so quickly that the soil will soon dry out? Or is it so dense that water cannot drain properly? Peat or vermiculite will help water retention; builder's sand or perlite will help drainage.

SKYLIGHTS AND
BUILT-IN PLANTERS

*Left: This apartment is packed
with young plants, and surprises.
Tradescantia, ivies, and commelina trail
from the balcony. Look closely and you'll
see a Dracaena surculosa (gold-dust
dracaena) and a two Cordyline terminalis.
Near the bar there's an Aspidistra
elatior (cast-iron plant), and below it,
an aglaonema (Chinese evergreen).
The narrow trough around the stairwell
has tradescantia, chlorophytum, African
violets, grape ivy, Boston ferns, English
ivy, and more.The ivies will soon
garland the stair rail, making a lush
hedge. Owner/architect: Alan Coles.*

SKYLIGHTS FOR
STAIRWELL/LIBRARY

*Right: Part library, part greenhouse, this
two-story gallery has a sloping glass
skylight that fills the house with light. A
Ficus retusa staked to a pole has a pot
half concealed by a kangaroo vine. The
red-painted metal staircase has two pots
of chlorophytum halfway up and Boston
fern suspended behind. It leads to the
upstairs with balcony-like openings for
catching the sun and growing more ferns
and vines. Owner/architect: David Fukui.*

**Tip: If you ever have a sick
plant that must be sprayed,
spray it and not the air you
breathe. Wrap the plant in
plastic, cut a small flap
through which to spray the
insecticide, and unwrap
after a day. A clean trash
can with a lid can also work.**

SWITCH-ON SUNLIGHT FOR A PLANT WALL

Their plant room is a living-room wall in an apartment, but cool energy-thrifty fluorescent bulbs, which give enough light even for plants to flower, make it a productive one. Everything is started from cuttings or seeds. Each shelf has a built-in waterproof tray with plastic egg crates to keep pots above water added for humidity. Over each tray are four 48-inch 40-watt tubes, on a 17-hour timer. Para-Wedge louvers banish the glare. Each shelf slides with a pulley for easy airing and tending. Among the plants are a peperomia (radiator plant), Rieger begonias, coleus, and Begonia boweri. On a bottom shelf are Aechmea Chantinii and spathiphyllum; on the floor are schefflera, Swedish ivy, and Epripremnum aureum (scindapsus). Owners/ designers: John H. and Penny Allan.

Tip: A thermometer set among your plants is a good idea. Ideally, use one that measures daily maximum-minimum temperatures. A hygrometer that measures relative humidity is also useful, as is a small electric fan that circulates air and helps keep plants comfortable and pest-free.

4
Containers and Centerpieces

Containers that suit the plant
and the room decoratively,
architecturally

Classic cylinders and cubes
that work well indoors and out

Compatible baskets for many
plants and decorating styles

Imaginative new ideas:
bark, moss, twigs

Plants as centerpieces:
live-in plants,
in-season plants, green
or flowering plants,
plants you can plant later
in a flowerpot or garden

While looking at the plants in this book, have you looked closely at the containers? You may have scarcely noticed them — for a good container, whether it holds the plant or conceals an inside pot, should not steal attention.

For some rooms, the pot or tub that comes with a plant is quite acceptable. Sometimes, however, something else is needed — something with shape, texture, color, or height that sets the plant off to its best advantage; something, too, that complements a well-decorated room. Proportion, scale, and harmony of materials enhance a plant; a highly ornamented or eye-catching container will usually detract. Classic shapes — spheres, cylinders, cubes, rectangles, or vase-like holders — are fail-safe and work well indoors or out. Containers that are mirrored, metal painted, fabric-covered, or of fiberglass are handsome in the right settings. And so are imaginative new ones with the natural look of bark, moss, or twigs.

An appropriate container will suit the plant and the eye. It will be both decorative and architecturally pleasing. A good choice can also be important to the plant's health, because the plant in an oversized pot or planter soon becomes over-watered and over-fed, and a too-small pot may force traumatic repotting.

An advantage of using slip-in containers is that they give balance to a shrubby or tall plant without actually increasing the volume of the soil around the roots. Baskets have an advantage in that they allow an interchange of air and moisture around the potted roots, just as clay pots do. A cachepot or jardiniere that prevents water from evaporating from the sides of a pot can be an asset for some moisture-loving plants — and for some gardeners, too, who prefer longer intervals between waterings.

Discretion is essential in selecting plants and containers to use as centerpieces. Small, low plants that can be moved to a dining table on short notice are suited to today's impromptu entertaining and can thriftily brighten party tables. For effective decorating, choosing the right container is second only to choosing the right plant.

A PERFECT MATCH

But, of course, this velvet-leaved gloxinia and long-eared rabbit seem made for each other. Even the flowers on his side look like a Sinningia speciosa's family crest. Whimsical containers must be used with care, but this one's terra-cotta earthiness, its flowerpot heritage, complements the plant it holds in shape, size, and texture. The inset shows orchids and clivia in baskets, and a pair of the large rabbits on a console.
Owner/designer: C. Z. Guest.

THE CONTAINER AS DECORATIVE ACCESSORY

Left: In this room with natural wood tones, tall covered baskets, and a chrome and wicker chair, the wide-weave basket for the Ficus retusa is a happy choice. The basket's pattern even picks up the geometric pattern of the rugs. Architect: Tony Cloughley. Interior designer: Alessandro Albrizzi.

THE CONTAINER AS ARCHITECTURE

Right: In this room with several large fishtail palms, and a flagstone wall and floor, a cube planter of matching stone is ideal for balance and is noncompetitive with clusters of wicker chairs. A small basket for cymbidiums is appropriate. Architect: John Mautner. Interior designer: Michael Taylor.

Tip: Large plants are hard to repot. To keep them healthy, pot in as coarse a soil as possible. Brick chunks, charcoal, perlite, and builder's sand improve aeration and drainage. Gravel at the bottom helps, too.

CLASSIC CYLINDERS INDOORS AND ON TERRACES

Above, below: Most plants – small, medium, or large – have an affinity for round containers, a shape as old as the urns in earliest garden history. Here, a pottery cylinder, seemingly woven, brims with Digitalis (foxglove). Next to it, a plastic tub on gliders holds Sea Foam white roses. In a kitchen designed by William and Jane Howard-Hammerstein, the Bambusa (bamboo) in its copper saucepan is a reminder that good containers are all around us. Look again at your unused ice bucket, cookie jar, or crock, all ready to be transformed.

COMPATIBLE EASY-GOING BASKETS AND CUBES

Above, below: A collection of baskets can unify a disparate collection of pot plants and fit into a simple or elegant room. Above: C.Z. Guest uses them for gloxinias, and laelia and cattleya orchids. Below: Cubes, like cylinders and baskets, are also classic forms, giving nice contrast to the softness of foliage and flowers. A half-cube triangle, ideal for a hallway corner, holds achillea. Next to it, a natural wood box full of garden plants such as astilbe, dianthus, and Armeria maritima, glides to catch the sun. A black cube in a metal cage contains spathiphyllum.

Tip: When shopping for baskets as containers, remember to allow space for air and easy lifting, and for a waterproof saucer to slip in and out. Measure the outside diameter of the pot and saucer, and add 2 inches all around. Add an extra inch at the top to conceal the rim.

THE NATURAL LOOK: BARK

Above: Bring nature indoors with imaginative containers of make-believe bark. This rough-textured but gracefully flared cachepot holds fresh-faced cineraria. Designer: Robert Webb.

DAVID MASSEY

THE NATURAL LOOK: MOSS

Above: Inside the green moss is a basket, and inside the basket is a pot of Primula polyantha. To make such a basket yourself, cut damp sheet moss and wrap the container like a package; then mist the moss to keep it green. Designer: Jean-Jacques Bloos.

THE NATURAL LOOK: TWIGS

Right: Another example of the natural look in small containers is this tall, narrow basket made of twigs tied with twine. It covers a small pot and supports the stems and leaves of fragrant, early-blooming paperwhite narcissus. Designer: Ronaldo Maia.

ERNST BEADLE

118

BRIGHT-COLORED CLOUD POTS

Above: This idea flings caution to the wind – the containers, gaily painted and eye-catching, take pastel house plants for a merry ride. But the point is that one needn't be hopelessly conventional about what goes with what. Plants and containers are to be enjoyed, and even house plants can decorate a garden for the day. These include African violets, gloxinias, and geraniums, which are in cloud pots by Norman Bacon.

Tip: Paperwhite narcissus can make a house fragrant throughout the winter. In fall, stash bulbs in a refrigerator or a 40° garage (5°C). Pot-up a few bulbs neck-high in gravel, every three weeks. Water, and place in a sunny spot to sprout — but move them out of the sun when they begin to bloom to make the flowers last longer.

119

HORST P.HORST

FRED LYON

LIVE-IN GREEN CENTERPIECE

Above: Decorating with plants to please family and guests is never a problem for plant lovers, however impromptu a feast may be. Even one small plant moved from window sill to table can make a meal seem festive. Here, a lined, waterproof basket with Selaginella (little club moss) is ringed with darker green Soleirolia Soleirolii (baby's-tears) on a travertine and cedar stump table. Interior designer: Michael Taylor.

IN-SEASON FLOWERING CENTERPIECE

Below: A tabletop garden, pretty enough to grace even a wedding breakfast, can come from anyone's window sill or fluorescent garden. You can also buy living plants to use first on the table and later in a plant room. Here, Primula obconica plants are tucked under sheet moss in a 19th-century silver plateau. Table setting by Inman Cook.

Tip: To pot plants temporarily in a basket or other shallow container, moisten the soil and gently remove plants from flats or pots. Slip them into separate bags or group them in foil- or plastic-lined containers. Sheet moss or shredded sphagnum around the edges will hold the plants together and help retain moisture.

PLANT-LATER CENTERPIECE

Left: In blue lacquered baskets, Bellis perennis (English daisies), and Lobelia Erinus decorate a table for the evening before they are moved to their new quarters – a garden or flowerpots – the next morning. The idea is to buy nursery-grown plants and enjoy them first in low foil-lined containers on the table. Architect: Robert Stern.

TABLE-TO-GARDEN CENTERPIECE

Below: Like a miniature meadow, a runner of growing grass and English daisies bisects a dinner-party table. On the window sill and buffet ledge, Begonia semperflorens and impatiens are still in their nursery-center boxes. Table setting by William Machado.

Tip: To make a meadow centerpiece, buy pre-cut sod. Place it on a runner of plastic to protect the table, and scoop out hollows to hold the flowers' plastic-wrapped soil balls.

5
Functions

Plants do so many things to decorate a room

They add softness and color, give any window a welcome view

Plants furnish oversized and lean rooms, bridge different levels, link different colors

Plants make flexible room dividers, double as sculpture, enhance doorways and walls, provide year-round greenery

Plants do many things

The deeper we plunge into a technological world with practical furnishings of glass, steel, and vinyl, the more we need the living, breathing grace of man's old companions on this earth, green plants and flowers. They are our link with nature. We even breathe the oxygen they replenish.

Indoor plants, like pets, also need us. They need shelter from heat and cold. They need light, air, food and water. They need grooming, sometimes doctoring. They will respond to good care with healthy growth and even a quiet congeniality. Plants are to be lived with and enjoyed — and as you extend a plant's life with good care, it will brighten yours.

Plants perform important functions in any room, both decoratively and architecturally. They can be relatively inexpensive substitutes for serious furniture, for knicknacks, and even for art. Remember our great-grandparents' tall corner cabinets gleaming with flowered teacups, urns filled with plumy peacock or ostrich feathers, and dark halls hung with landscape tapestries? Now, with our bigger windows and improved light sources, we grow tall green plants instead. Plants replace heavy curtains, providing privacy and filtering light. They serve as walls, room dividers, and balusters for steps, bridging levels and giving balance. They provide pattern and texture and color. They offer year-round greenery, creating an outdoorsy feeling whatever the weather.

The more you learn about plants' proportions, needs, and characteristics (including whether they are forgiving or imperious), and the more you analyze the rooms in this book and in your own home, the better indoor gardener you will become. Knowledge comes with experience, and experience often comes with mistakes — but there isn't an expert who hasn't learned by daring to try something new.

Indoor plants have never been more popular or more accessible, so make the most of nature's gifts from woodland and garden, desert and jungle. Decorate with plants.

PLANTS ADD SOFTNESS AND COLORS

To create the illusion of great space in a two-room apartment, furniture and colors were kept at a minimum. The conversation area consists of two sofas and a bed, all upholstered in heavy white cotton canvas. The bed has wide ledges cushioned with foam rubber. A bamboo coffee table serves both sofas and bed. A painting by the owner, along with a few pillows, adds minimal color. Two Howea Belmoreana palms provide great sweeps of softness and color, color that is reflected in the white-on-white mirror. Owner/designer: Sam Verts.

PLANTS TEMPER LIGHT

Without blocking the view or limiting the light, these three Ficus benjamina trees soften harsh light that could fade fabric and a glare that could make this room less inviting. The room is Spanish Colonial, but not heavily done. White goldfish swim in blue linen ponds; the sofa and chair seats are cobalt blue. The furniture is wicker, reed, and bleached oak. A Boston fern, cut hydrangeas, and cut leaves add other touches of greenery. The fern's planter echoes the blue and white of the Chinese porcelain ginger jar and table plates. Interior designer: Michael Taylor.

Tip: Plants in bright light require more food than plants in low light, and all plants will need bigger helpings during spring and summer's active growth than during fall and winter, when the plants are coasting. Because manufacturers' formulas are for plants at their peak, dilute in winter, or if you feed often.

CHARLES ASHLEY

ERNST BEADLE

TED HARDIN

PLANTS FURNISH OVERSIZED ROOMS

In this remodeled barn, a Ficus benjamina 'Exotica' that would threaten any other ceiling creates a leafy canopy for a chaise longue near a sunny window. By scaling down the ceiling, it makes not only an inviting spot for reading or napping but a well-proportioned link with the outdoors. Fronds of Boston fern soften the base of the tree. The Palladian window was found at a junkyard and installed by the barn's carpenter, Henry Booth. Owner/designer: Michael Wager.

Tip: Two plants can live as cheaply as one in the same container if their needs are compatible. Ficus and ferns, for instance, both like dappled light and ample moisture. Boston ferns and asparagus ferns make pretty ruffs for trees.

Tip: Everybody loves ivy, including tiny red spider mites that make dusty webs and drain the leaves of nutrients. To foil them, shower the leaves twice a week if you can — mites do their dirty work in hot, dry places. If you see a cottony deposit on any plant, that's a mealy bug. Remove it with a swab dipped in alcohol, even gin.

PLANTS GENTLE HARD SURFACES

Above: Down stone steps, past newly plastered stone walls, to a tile floor and tile table: what might have been the corner of an uninviting cellar is now a welcoming room with soft cushions and soft green plants — a Sedum mexicanum and selaginella. This was an old stable on the ground level of a farmhouse that has been restored by Robert Courtright and Bruno Romeda.

PLANTS FURNISH LEAN ROOMS

Right: The white of the fireplace was extended to the ceiling in a giant supergraphic canopy over a cable-spool table, a sofa, and simple wicker pieces. The rest of the room is furnished with plants: English ivy, a grouping of podocarpus, Ficus retusa, and Dracaena fragrans. Interior designer: John F. Saladino, Inc.

PLANTS ENRICH GEOMETRIC FORMS

Left: In this apartment a spiral staircase goes up a cylinder lined with silvery Mylar. Wallboard was pierced to create circular windows, which are reflected in a mirrored wall. Lucite cubes, low rectangular furniture, and a bull's-eye rug add more contemporary geometry. Along the reflecting wall a shelf of dieffenbachias and scheffleras lends rich pattern and color. Architect: Stanley Tigerman and Associates.

Tip: Moving? Don't water if the trip's a short one — it makes pots heavy to carry. Put big cleaning bags over the heads of trees. If there's a nip in the air, wrap plants in newspapers. Twist trailing plants around tissue paper to keep them from tangling.

ROBERT LAUTMAN

PLANTS ADD A TOUCH OF EDEN

Above: Privacy is not a problem here in this island bedroom-bath, but even where it is, a bower of plants does wonders to buffer the outside world. Screening the tub are three tall palms — Arecastrum Romanzoffianum, plus lacy Dizygotheca elegantissima, a Pittosporum Tobira — and cattleya orchids. Architect: Hugh Newell Jacobsen. Interior designer: Edward Benesch.

TOM YEE

PLANTS REPLACE INTERIOR WALLS

Left: Three baskets above a sunken living room serve as an airy divider between the sitting area and raised dining area. One of the baskets is a cachepot for an areca palm. The colors and textures were inspired by Japanese kabuki theater — wood tones (the interior is fir-timbered), straw, black floor, little islands of color, and just one touch of greenery. Architect: Norman Jaffe.

PLANTS INDICATE CHANGES IN LEVELS

Right: Bridging the level between a hall and living room, containers of Chamaedorea elegans (parlor palm) and Boston fern guard an open hallway below. A Zebrina pendula at the end of a bench marks a short flight of stairs. On the upper level a podocarpus and a Ficus benjamina flank the fireplace but are kept safely away from the hearth. It's all wonderfully soothing to the eye and leads it to the window-framed sea meadow beyond. Architect: Norman Jaffe.

Tip: In the dark about plants' light requirements? There are vast differences between such terms as high-light intensity, indirect light, and low light. High light is sun, or its fluorescent equivalent; indirect light (bright shade) means near but not in sunlight; and low light is farther still from a light source. Many plants that tolerate low light do better in indirect medium light.

PLANTS LINK DIFFERENT LEVELS

Left: What once was an unfinished attic over a living room is now a plant-filled balcony with a music room at one end. Easy grape ivy is set in copper-lined troughs. There's a Rhapis excelsa palm at the top and a Ficus benjamina below. To give an encore to the skylights at night, swivel spotlights are beamed at panels opposite their own. Lights under the balcony illuminate a Sam Gilliam painting and plants below. Interior designer: Ann Hartman.

PLANTS PROVIDE COLOR LINKS

Right: Just one heart-leaved Philodendron scandens oxycardium spilling from the yellow balcony above a green sofa and chairs adds emphasis to the color scheme, and grace to the room. A chlorophytum and another philodendron near the window and stereo system repeat the color and pattern of the leafy pillows on the sofa. Architect: Robert Whitton.

Tip: Some music lovers swear plants do best to the strains of classical music and suffer when they hear loud rock. Some botanists say people who love good music are attentive at home while listening, and so their plants stay happy, too.

PLANTS MAKE ILLUSIONARY WALLS

Left: A Ficus benjamina and hanging macramé baskets create a sense of enclosure for a loft in a new barn-shaped house. Other plants, including a Philodendron Selloum, are banked near the sliding doors of a double-paned south-facing window wall. Watering is an easy reach from the loft level, and the unwaxed quarry-tile floor is spillproof. Chrysanthemums are in the foreground. Architect: Edmund Stevens.

PLANTS MAKE FLEXIBLE DIVIDERS

Above: A tubbed areca palm and a small kentia palm in a basket divide the living and dining areas of this light-filled gallery. The wing was added at the back of a Georgian house, and floor vents spray the tinted glass with cool air. The flowers on the table are Kalanchoe flammea. Architect: Charles Tapley and Associates.

Tip: Pebbles in a watertight tray under a pot are a good way to boost humidity in a sunny area or in any house where watering must be a weekend matter. A canister lid or pizza pan makes a simple and practical plant tray.

PLANTS BRIDGE OUTDOORS, INDOORS

Left: From the sofa in this family room, you can look at a garden on both sides of the picture window. The garden inside includes a tubbed monstera, which in turn provides balance for the tall Ficus retusa at the other end of the room. The painting is by Pedro Coronel. Architect: Charles Tapley and Associates.

PLANTS BRIDGE SPATIAL DIFFERENCES

Above and right: A beach cottage with views of the sea and of pine trees has raised platforms by the sofa, accented by Swedish ivy and a finely cut Philodendron bipinnatifidum. Steps between the living room and dining area are defined by Dracaena fragrans and Pilea microphylla (artillery plant). Architects: Robert Stern and John Hagmann.

Tip: Small plants look best and do better if grouped together. As each adds moisture to the air, they raise each other's humidity level. If clay pots are watered elsewhere they can sit on the floor, but to be sure they're moisture-proof, seal the bottoms with clear nail polish.

PLANTS ACCENT ARCHITECTURAL FEATURES

Above: This large room with uncurtained windows and glass-door window walls was once a two-story chicken house. Now plants accent the room's 17-foot height and interesting architectural details. Two asparagus ferns pattern a ledge behind a structural pole, which is accented by Swedish ivy suspended on fishline. On a corner platform, soft greenery; on a modular coffee table, another Swedish ivy. For Albert Hamowy by designer James G. Rogers III.

PLANTS ADD PATTERN TO WALLS

Right: This small, boxlike room was changed into a light-filled library/sitting room when a wall was pushed out four feet and opened onto a treetop balcony with sliding glass doors. In a sheltered corner, an areca palm casts its green fronds and elegant shadows on the new wall. It is dramatized at night by floodlights. For Molly Bogounoff by architect Hans Ullrich Scharnberg.

Tip: For hanging plants, nothing beats sturdy, almost-invisible nylon fishline, the 40-pound test or more. It's a good idea, too, to use fishline as back-up support for macramé and leather thongs that can deteriorate in time. You can get it at hardware and sporting-goods shops.

TOM YEE

PLANTS DOUBLE AS BALUSTERS

In this poolside pavilion, seasonal plants mark the break between the lower level, with yellow vinyl banquettes, and the upper level, for after-swim conversation and games. Marguerites and Swedish ivy are the markers. A Boston fern also flanks the banquette, and an Alsophila Cooperi stands near the skylighted hearth. Air-cooled in summer, the two areas are closed off by glass doors; they slide into side pockets from grooves in the beams and floors. Architects: Robert Stern and John Hagmann.

Tip: Plants like cool rooms in summer just as people do. They don't object to air conditioning if they're not in a blast, but it does draw moisture from the air, soil, and leaves, so double up on your misting. You don't want your plants to be dehydrated.

144

Tip: A well-balanced watering can with a long nose and a sprinkler(called a rose) is an essential tool for the indoor gardener who wants to reach pots in back rows or up high with ease and accuracy.

PLANTS MAKE THE MOST OF A SMALL WINDOW

Above: A window greenhouse stretches window-sill space for a herb garden in a laundry room. Basil, parsley, thyme, and others bask in the three-way light. Cabinet tops and a nearby sink provide a handy potting bench for petunias and other plants. Owner/designer: Mrs. Quaintance Mason.

PLANTS CURTAIN A BAY WINDOW

Right: A bay window reaching out to scoop up sun is curtained by plants near a dining area. Macramé baskets suspend a chlorophytum and grape ivy above an array of floor plants: Ficus benjamina, Acalypha Wilkesiana 'Macafeeana' (copperleaf), chrysanthemums, Alsophilia Cooperi, and gold-dust dracaena. All are set on tile near an American-Indian rug. Architect: Edmund Stevens.

PLANTS DOUBLE AS SCULPTURE

Left and right, above: In this long, lean living room (at left you look into it, and at right you look out), a window wall has year-round interest. A multi-trunked Dracaena fragrans 'Massangeana' balances a group of Euphorbia ingens. Matching plants could have been a bore, while this combination makes the most of the glass-wall view. Architect: Myron Goldfinger.

PLANTS MAKE PICTURES OF WINDOWS

Right, below: A barn turned painter's studio lets plants share the good light. One bracing rod added during remodeling holds hanging baskets. A plank set on wood blocks at the window's base supports other plants, including Abutilon megapotamicum 'Variegata' (flowering maple), with green-leaved varieties in bloom above it. Owner/artist: Kenneth Noland.

Tip: To move a plant on an uncarpeted floor, save your back by keeping it on an old piece of rug, pile-side down, for easy sliding.

PIER GIORGIO SCLARANDIS   HORST P. HORST

PLANTS PROVIDE VISUAL BALANCE

Left: Orchids and trees on each side of the fireplace anchor this soaring room in a remodeled 1920s house. In another era, massive armoires or bookshelves might have been chosen for such baronial dimensions, but for contemporary taste, plants are the winners hands down. The trees are Japanese maples, brought in for the season, then replaced by year-round ficus. The orchids are cymbidiums. The charcoal drawing is by Ann Rhodin. Owners/designers: Jeffrey and Jasmine Lindsay.

PLANTS REPEAT COLORS AND SHAPES

Right: In this stairway with brick arches on the inside, camellia trees against the cool arched windows of the outer wall give a sense of security and balance. They make the steps more than just a climb or descent; they make them an aesthetic experience. The saucers here are pig feeders from a farm store. The low green plants are English ivy. Architect: I. W. Colburn.

Tip: It's almost impossible to empty a saucer if you over-water a big plant. A basting syringe, or a sponge, and handy pail could come to the rescue.

PLANTS MASK CITY VIEWS

Left: A glassed partition in this apartment keeps plants together near the windows, creating a leafy view. The plants sit on a platform around a small sunken pool that maintains high humidity. Among the plants: pink hyacinths and cyclamen, Dracaena fragrans 'Massangeana,' Alsophila Cooperi, schefflera, a Ficus benjamina, and Philodendron scandens oxycardium. Owner/designer: Mrs. Peter Millard.

PLANTS PROVIDE YEAR-ROUND GREENERY

Above: To widen a narrow apartment living room and to provide a fresh green view, windows were hung with horizontal aluminum blinds flanked by mirror panels. They add the gleam, and plants add the view: Philodendron Selloum, Ficus benjamina, Davallia solida ferns, and in season, white cyclamen and paperwhites. Interior designers: Mica Ertegün and Chessy Rayner of MAC II.

Tip: Measure the rooms you plan to decorate and measure the plants you plan to buy. Remember to allow for growth. A happy plant can grow in height and girth if you pick the right plant for the right place.

Caring for Your Plants

BOTANICAL NAME (and pronunciation of genus)	COMMON NAME	GROWTH REQUIREMENTS	BOOK PAGE
Abutilon megapotamicum (ab-yew´-til-on)	Flowering maple	Sun Moist Tall	**149**
Abutilon megapotamicum 'Variegata'	Flowering maple (variegated)	Sun Moist	**149**
Acalypha Wilkesiana 'Macafeeana' (ak-al-lye´-fuh)	Copperleaf	Sun Moist	**147**
Achimenes (ak-kim´-in-eez)		Indirect Moist	**53**
Aechmea Chantinii (eek´-mee-uh)		Indirect Dry *	**111**
Aechmea fasciata	Urn plant	Indirect Dry *	**31, 44, 69, 93**
Aeschynanthus Trichosporum (esk-in-anth´-us)		Indirect Moist	**99, 104**
Aglaonema modestum (ag-lay-oh-nee´-muh)	Chinese evergreen	Low Moist to dry	**108**
Alsophila Cooperi (al-soff´-il-uh)	Tree fern	Indirect Wet	**33, 144-45, 147, 152**
Ananas comosus (an-nan´-ass)	Pineapple	Sun Moist	**72**
Anthurium (an-thew´-ree-um)	Tailflower, Flamingo lily	Low Wet	**97**
Arecastrum Romanzoffianum (ar-ek-kast´-rum)	Queen palm	Indirect Wet Tall	**133**
Asparagus densiflorus 'Myers' (ass-pear´-uh-gus)	Asparagus fern	Indirect Moist	**9, 94**
Asparagus densiflorus 'Sprengeri'	Asparagus fern	Indirect Moist	**21, 43, 55, 56-57, 61, 88, 143**
Asparagus setaceus plumosus	Asparagus fern	Indirect Moist	**21, 44, 78, 94**
Aspidistra elatior (ass-pid-dist´-ruh)	Cast-iron plant, Barroom plant	Low Moist *	**108, 131**
Asplenium bulbiferum (ass-pleen´-ee-um)	Mother fern, Hen-and-chickens fern	Low Moist	**102**
Asplenium nidus	Bird's-nest fern	Low Moist	**34, 102**
Azalea/Rhododendron (az-zay´-lee-uh)	Azalea	Sun Wet Cool	**18, 19**
Bambusa (bam-bew´-suh)	Bamboo	Sun Moist Tall	**116**
Begonia (beg-gon´-nee-uh)	Angel wing	Indirect Moist	**71, 96**
Begonia Boweri	Eyelash begonia	Indirect Moist	**110**
Begonia x hiemalis 'Rieger'	Rieger begonia	Indirect Moist	**41, 55, 73, 79, 110**
Begonia x rex-cultorum	Rex begonia	Indirect Moist	**100**
Begonia x semperflorens-cultorum	Wax begonia	Indirect Moist	**19, 103, 123**
Beloperone guttata (bel-op-er-oh´-nee)	Shrimp plant	Sun Dry	**58**
Bougainvillea Buttiana (boo-gin-vil´-ee-uh)	Bougainvillea	Sun Dry	**92**
Brassaia actinophylla (brass´-ee-uh)	Schefflera, Australian umbrella tree	Sun Dry Tall *	**20, 39, 43, 44, 111, 132, 152**

BOTANICAL NAME (and pronunciation of genus)	COMMON NAME	GROWTH REQUIREMENTS	BOOK PAGE
Bromelia serra 'Variegata' (bro-me-li-a)		Sun Moist	**97**
Caladium (kay-lay-dee-um)	Elephant's-ear	Indirect Moist	**99, 100**
Calceolaria crenatiflora (kal-see-oh-lay-ree-uh)	Slipperwort, Pocketbook flower	Indirect Dry Cool G	**12, 17, 83**
Camellia japonica (kam-meel-ee-uh)	Camellia	Indirect Wet Cool Tall	**103, 151**
Capsicum (kap-si-kum)	Pepper	Sun Moist	**59**
Caryota mitis (kare-ee-oh-tuh)	Burmese fishtail palm	Indirect Wet Tall *	**23, 25, 65, 115**
Cassia (kass-ee-uh)	Senna, Shower tree	Sun Moist Tall	**72**
Cattleya (kat-lee-uh)	Corsage orchid	Indirect Dry	**74, 113, 117, 133**
Cereus (seer-ee-us)		Sun Dry	**33**
Chamaedorea elegans (kam-ee-doh-ree-uh)	Parlor palm, Neanthe bella	Low Moist	**135**
Chamaedorea erumpens	Bamboo palm	Low Moist Tall *	**106**
Chlorophytum comosum (kloh-roff-ite-um)	Spider plant	Indirect Moist *	**21, 71, 137**
Chlorophytum comosum 'Vittatum'	Spider plant (white-striped)	Indirect Moist *	**33, 44, 97, 108, 109, 147**
Chrysalidocarpus lutescens (kriss-al-id-oh-karp-us)	Areca palm, Yellow butterfly palm	Indirect Wet Tall *	**39, 96, 98, 134, 139, 142**
Chrysanthemum frutescens (kriss-anth-em-um)	Marguerite, Paris daisy	Sun Moist Cool G	**16, 145**
Chrysanthemum x morifolium	Florist's chrysanthemum	Sun Moist Cool G	**13, 33, 43, 45, 46, 48 52, 55, 58, 82, 98, 100, 111, 114, 138, 142, 147**
Cissus antarctica (siss-us)	Kangaroo vine	Indirect Dry to moist *	**73, 81, 85, 109**
Cissus rhombifolia	Grape ivy	Indirect Dry to moist *	**15, 20, 35, 42, 43, 50, 51, 54, 56-57, 88, 102, 108, 136, 147**
Citrofortunella x mitis (sit-ro-for-tew-nell-uh)	Calamondin orange	Sun Dry Cool	**10, 104**
Citrus aurantiifolia (sit-rus)	Lime	Sun Dry Cool	**104**
Citrus Limon 'Meyer'	Lemon	Sun Dry Cool	**84**
Citrus x limonia	Otaheite orange	Sun Dry Cool	**84**
Citrus sinensis	Sweet orange	Sun Dry Cool Tall	**82**

LEGEND:
Sun at least half day, or 12 hours of fluorescent light daily   **Indirect** good light   **Low** light tolerant   **Dry** between waterings   **Moist** to the touch between waterings   **Wet** frequent waterings, or grows in water   **Cool** nights and days 50°–65°F (10°–18°C). Other plants tolerate or prefer warmer range, 65°–75°F (18°–24°C)   **Tall** grows over 5 feet indoors without support   **G** greenhouse plants, seasonal, prefer low light in bloom   * Extra easy   **x** Sign for hybrid

NOTE: If no common name is listed, the botanical name is used. If no accent is given in the genus pronounciation, each syllable receives equal stress.

BOTANICAL NAME (and pronunciation of genus)	COMMON NAME	GROWTH REQUIREMENTS		BOOK PAGE
Clivia miniata (klye-vee-uh)	Kaffir lily	Indirect Dry		66, 113
Coccoloba Uvifera (kok-kol-oh-buh)	Sea grape	Sun to indirect Moist *		77
Codiaeum variegatum (koh-dih-ee-um)	Croton	Sun Moist		78, 100
Coffea arabica (koff-ee-uh)	Arabian coffee	Indirect Moist Tall		58
Coleus (koh-lee-us)	Flame nettle, Painted leaves	Sun Moist *		110
Colocasia esculenta (kol-oh-kay-see-uh)	Elephant's-ear, Taro	Indirect Wet		20
Commelina (kom-el-lye-nuh)	Day flower	Indirect Moist		108
Cordyline australis (kor-dil-lye-nee)	Giant dracaena, Fountain dracaena	Indirect Moist to Dry Tall		89, 106
Cordyline terminalis	Ti, Good luck plant	Indirect Moist Tall		97, 108
Crassula argentea (krass-yew-luh)	Jade tree	Sun to indirect Dry *		33, 72, 143
Cussonia spicata (kew-son-ee-uh)		Indirect Moist		37
Cycas revoluta (sye-kass)	Sago palm	Indirect Dry Tall *		92
Cyclamen persicum (sik-lam-en)		Indirect Moist Cool	G	13, 152, 153
Cymbidium (sim-bid-ee-um)	Cymbidium orchid	Indirect Moist Cool		80, 115, 150
Cyperus alternifolius (sye-peer-us)	Umbrella plant	Indirect Wet *		74-75
Cyperus alternifolius 'Gracilis'	Paper plant, Bulrush	Indirect Wet *		74-75
Cyperus Papyrus	Rabbit's-foot fern	Indirect Wet *		33
Davallia fejeensis (dav-val-lee-uh)		Low Moist *		63
Davallia solida	Dendrobium orchid	Low Moist *		153
Dendrobium (den-droh-bee-um)	Dumb cane	Indirect Dry		104
Dieffenbachia maculata 'Jenmannii' (deef-en-bak-ee-uh)		Indirect Dry *		18. 21, 30, 44, 104, 132
Dieffenbachia maculata 'Rudolph Roehrs'	False aralia, Finger aralia	Indirect Dry *		97
Dizygotheca elegantissima (dye-zye-goh-theek-uh)		Indirect Moist Tall		133
Dracaena cincta (dras-seen-uh)	Dracaena marginata	Indirect Moist to Dry Tall *		19, 33, 67, 103
Dracaena deremensis 'Warneckii'		Indirect Moist to dry *		84
Dracaena fragrans	Corn plant	Indirect Moist to Dry Tall *		19, 76, 131, 141
Dracaena fragrans 'Massangeana'	Corn plant (yellow-striped)	Indirect Moist to Dry Tall *		43, 103, 148, 152
Dracaena surculosa	Gold-dust dracaena	Indirect Moist to dry *		108, 147
Eichornia crassipes (ike-horn-ee-uh)	Water hyacinth	Indirect Wet		74
Epripremnum aureum (ep-ree-prem-num)	Scindapsus aureus, Pothos	Indirect Moist to dry *		111
Eucomis comosa (yew-kom-iss)	Pineapple flower	Sun Moist		69
Euphorbia canariensis (yew-forb-ee-uh)		Sun Dry		30
Euphorbia ingens		Sun Dry Tall		149
Euphorbia Milii	Crown-of-thorns	Sun Moist *		64

BOTANICAL NAME (and pronunciation of genus)	COMMON NAME	GROWTH REQUIREMENTS	BOOK PAGE
Euphorbia Tirucalli	Pencil tree	Sun Dry Tall *	**81**
Fatshedera x Lizei (fats-hed´-e-ruh)	Aralia ivy, Tree ivy	Indirect Moist Cool	**55**
Fatsia japonica (fats´-see-uh)		Indirect Moist Cool	**55**
Ficus benjamina (fye´-kus)	Weeping fig, Java fig	Indirect Moist Tall *	**10, 18, 20, 22, 33, 36, 40, 47, 49, 62, 68, 69, 72, 96, 97, 104, 126-27, 128, 135, 136, 138, 144, 147, 152, 153**
Ficus benjamina 'Exotica'	Exotic fig	Indirect Moist Tall *	**43, 95, 105, 128**
Ficus elastica	Rubber plant	Indirect Moist Tall *	**21**
Ficus lyrata	Fiddle-leaf fig	Indirect Moist Tall	**10**
Ficus retusa	Indian laurel	Indirect Moist Tall *	**9, 12, 13, 18, 22, 38, 39, 42, 52, 63, 98, 107, 109, 114, 131, 140**
Gardenia (gar-deen´-eh-uh)		Sun Moist	**42**
Grevillea robusta (grev-vill´-ee-uh)	Silky oak	Sun Dry Tall	**76**
Hedera Helix (hed´-er-uh)	English ivy	Sun to indirect Moist Cool	**35, 44, 92, 108, 131, 151**
Herbs	Basil, Chives, Dill, Parsley, Sorrel, Thyme	Sun Moist to dry	**53, 57, 59, 146**
Hippeastrum (hip-pee-ast´-rum)	Amaryllis	Sun Moist	**15, 102**
Howea Belmoreana (how´-ee-uh)	Belmore sentry palm	Indirect Moist Tall *	**125**
Howea Forsterana	Kentia palm, Sentry palm	Indirect Moist Tall *	**41, 107, 139**
Hyacinthus orientalis (hye-uh-sinth´-us)	Dutch hyacinth	Sun Moist Cool	**11, 77, 152**
Hydrangea macrophylla (hye-drayn´-jee-uh)	Hydrangea, Hortensia	Sun Wet G	**19, 23, 24, 25, 126**
Impatiens Wallerana (im-pay´-shee-enz)	Busy Lizzy, Sultana	Sun to indirect Moist *	**47, 56, 67, 79, 122, 123**
Iresine Lindenii (eye-res-sye´-nee)	Bloodleaf	Sun Moist	**10**
Kalanchoe flammea (kal-an-koh-ee)		Sun Dry *	**139**
Laelia (lee´-lee-uh)	Laelia orchid	Indirect Dry Cool	**117**
Licuala grandis (lik-yew-ay´-luh)	Small fan palm	Indirect Moist	**76**
Maranta leuconeura (mar-rant´-uh)	Prayer plant	Indirect Moist	**96**
Miltonia (mil-toh´-nee-uh)	Pansy orchid	Low Moist Cool	**27, 101**
Monstera deliciosa (mon-ster´-uh)	Split-leaf philodendron	Indirect Moist *	**19, 104, 140**
Muscari (muss-kar´-eye)	Grape hyacinth	Sun Wet Cool	**11**
Narcissus (nar-sis´-us)	Daffodil	Sun Moist Cool	**11, 35, 36, 102, 118, 153**
Narcissus Tazetta	Paperwhite	Sun Moist Cool	**102, 118, 153**
Narcissus Tazetta 'Soleil d'or'		Sun Moist Cool	**102**

BOTANICAL NAME (and pronunciation of genus)	COMMON NAME	GROWTH REQUIREMENTS	BOOK PAGE
Neoregelia Carolinae 'Tricolor' (nee-oh-rej-eel-ee-uh)		Indirect Moist *	22
Nephrolepis exaltata 'Bostoniensis' (nef-frol-ep-iss)	Boston fern	Indirect Moist *	10, 26, 33, 37, 40, 42, 44 45, 48, 52, 56-57, 67, 80, 96, 97, 100, 103, 105, 107, 108, 109, 126, 128, 135, 144-45
Nerine (nee-rye-nee)		Sun Dry Cool	44
Nerium Oleander (neer-ee-um)	Oleander, Rosebay	Sun Moist Tall *	96, 100
Nymphaea (nim-fee-uh)	Water lily	Sun Wet	74
Oncidium (on-sid-ee-um)	Dancing-lady orchid	Indirect Dry Cool	99, 104
Oxalis (ox-al-is)	Wood sorrel	Sun Dry Cool	85
Pandanus Veitchii (pan-day-nus)	Screw pine	Indirect Dry *	18
Pandanus Veitchii 'Compacta'		Indirect Dry *	18, 37
Paphiopedilum (pap-ee-oh-ped-il-um)	Lady-slipper orchid	Low Moist	74, 101, 103
Passiflora (pas-if-floh-ruh)	Passionflower	Sun Moist	84, 99
Pelargonium x hortorum (pel-ahr-goh-nee-um)	Geranium	Sun Dry Cool	14, 42, 46, 49, 79, 84, 100, 103, 104, 119
Pelargonium peltatum	Ivy geranium	Sun Dry Cool	56, 57, 84, 88, 96
Peperomia (pep-er-roh-mee-uh)		Indirect Dry *	110
Persea americana (per-see-a)	Avocado	Sun to indirect Moist	10, 21
Phalaenopsis (fal-ee-nops-iss)	Moth orchid	Low Moist	58, 104
Philodendron 'Barryi' (fil-oh-den-dron)		Sun to indirect Moist *	99
Philodendron bipinnatifidum		Sun to indirect Moist *	191
Philodendron cordatum	Heart-leaf philodendron	Indirect Moist *	101
Philodendron lacerum		Indirect Moist *	43
Philodendron scandens	Heart-leaf philodendron	Indirect Moist *	97
Philodendron scandens oxycardium	Parlor ivy, Common philodendron	Indirect Moist *	49, 70, 71, 137, 152
Philodendron Selloum		Sun to indirect Moist	89, 97, 138, 153
Phoenix canariensis (fee-nix)	Canary date palm	Sun Wet Cool Tall *	97
Phormium tenax (form-ee-um)	New Zealand flax	Sun Moist *	28
Pilea microphylla (pi-le-a)	Artillery plant	Indirect Moist *	141
Pittosporum Tobira (Pit-tosp-or-um)		Sun Dry Cool *	133
x Pityrogramma hybrida (pit-ihr-oh-gram-uh)	Silver fern, gold fern	Indirect Moist Cool	63
Platycerium bifurcatum (plat-iss-seer-ee-um)	Staghorn fern	Indirect Moist	99
Plectranthus australis (plek-tranth-us)	Swedish ivy	Indirect Moist *	20, 42, 44, 54, 85, 111, 141, 143, 145
Podocarpus macrophyllus (pod-oh-karp-us)	Southern yew, Buddhist pine	Sun to indirect Moist Cool Tall	60, 131, 135

BOTANICAL NAME (and pronunciation of genus)	COMMON NAME	GROWTH REQUIREMENTS	BOOK PAGE
Polypodium aureum (pol-ip-poh´-dee-um)	Hare's-foot fern	Indirect Moist *	77
Polypodium aureum arecolatum		Indirect Moist *	49
Polypodium scolopendria		Indirect Moist	72
Polypodium subauriculatum	Jointed fern	Indirect Moist	80
Polyscias Balfouriana (pol-liss´-ee-us)	Balfour Aralia	Sun Moist Tall	34, 76, 147
Primula obconica (prim´-yew-luh)	German primrose	Indirect Moist Cool G	19, 36, 121
Primula polyantha	Primrose, Polyanthus	Indirect Wet Cool G	36, 50, 78, 118
Pteris cretica (tehr´-iss)	Cretan brake, Table fern	Low Moist *	99
Rhapis excelsa (ray´-pis)	Lady palm	Indirect Wet	136
Rhoicissus capensis (roh´-zuh)	Cape grape	Indirect Dry	21, 44, 45
Rosa (rho-ee-siss´-us)	Rose	Sun Moist	96, 116
Rosmarinus officinalis 'Prostratus' (ross-muh-rye´-nus)	Prostrate rosemary	Sun Moist *	102
Saintpaulia ionantha (saint-paul´-ee-uh)	African violet	Indirect Moist	44, 53, 108, 119
Schlumbergera Bridgesii (schlum-ber-jeer´-uh)	Christmas cactus	Indirect Moist to dry Cool *	61
Sedum griseum (seed´-um)		Sun Dry *	72
Sedum mexicanum		Sun Dry *	130
Selaginella (sel-uh-jin-nell´-uh)	Little club moss	Low Moist	120, 130
Senecio cruentus (sen-nee´-shee-oh)	Cineraria	Sun to indirect Moist Cool G	98, 118
Sinningia speciosa (sin-nin´-jee-uh)	Gloxinia	Indirect Moist	9, 11, 68, 96, 102, 113, 117, 119
Solanum Pseudocapsicum (so-lay´-num)	Jerusalem cherry	Sun Dry	98
Soleirolia Soleirolii (soh-lee-roh´-lee-uh)	Baby's-tears, Helxine	Indirect Moist	120
Spathiphyllum 'Clevelandii' (spath-if-fill´-um)		Low Wet *	44, 76, 111, 117
Strelitzia reginae (strel-itt´-see-uh)	Bird-of-paradise	Sun Dry	31
Thalia dealbata (thay´-lee-uh)		Sun Wet	74-75
Tolmiea Menziesii (tol-mee-ee´-uh)	Pickaback plant, Piggyback	Indirect Moist Cool *	71
Tradescantia albiflora (trad-es-kant´-ee-uh)	Wandering Jew, Inch plant	Indirect Dry *	20, 108
Tripogandra multiflora (trip-o-gan´-druh)	Fern-leaf inch plant	Indirect Dry *	48, 85
Tulipa (tew´-lip-uh)	Tulip	Sun Moist Cool	11, 12, 38, 102
Vriesea (vree´-zee-uh)		Indirect Dry	29
Yucca (yukk´-uh)		Sun Dry	30
Zebrina pendula (zeb-rye´-nuh)	Wandering Jew, Inch plant	Indirect Moist *	42, 135

Outdoor Plants and Cut Flowers Temporarily Indoors

BOTANICAL NAME (and pronunciation of genus)	COMMON NAME	MAINTENANCE REQUIREMENTS		BOOK PAGE
Acer japonicum (ay´-ser)	Japanese maple	Indirect to low	Moist	**150**
Achillea filipendulina (ak-il-lee´-uh)	Fern-leaf yarrow	Indirect to low	Moist	**117**
Antirrhinum (an-tihr-rye´-num)	Snapdragon	Indirect to low	Fresh water	**140**
Armeria maritima (arm-meer´-ee-uh)	Thrift, Sea pink	Indirect to low	Moist	**117**
Astilbe (ass-till´-bee)	Spiraea	Indirect to low	Moist	**117**
Bellis perennis (bell´-iss)	English daisy	Indirect to low	Moist	**122, 123**
Browallia (broh-wal´-lee-uh)		Indirect to low	Moist	**47**
Coreopsis (koh-ree-op´-siss)	Tickseed	Indirect to low	Fresh water	**128, 129**
Cornus florida (korn´-us)	Flowering dogwood	Indirect to low Crush stems to take water	Fresh water	**66**
Cortaderia (kor-ta-deer´-ee-uh)	Pampas grass	Indirect to low	No water	**147**
Dahlia (dahl´-yuh)		Indirect to low	Fresh water	**39**
Daucus Carota (daw´-kus)	Queen-Anne's-lace	Indirect to low	Fresh water	**9, 128**
Dianthus (dye-anth´-us)	Pink	Indirect to low	Moist to dry	**117**
Digitalis purpurea (dij-it-tay´-liss)	Common foxglove	Indirect to low	Moist	**116**
Forsythia (for-sith´-ee-uh)	Golden-bells	Indirect to low Crush stems to take water	Fresh water	**35**
Hydrangea macrophylla (hye-drayn´-jee-uh)	Hortensia	Indirect to low	Fresh water	**127**
Lilium speciosum 'Rubrum' (lill´-ee-um)	Lily	Indirect to low	Fresh water	**54**
Lobelia Erinus (loh-beel´-ee-uh)	Edging lobelia	Indirect to low	Moist	**122**
Paeonia (pay-oh´-nee-ah)	Peony	Indirect to low	Fresh water	**25**
Petunia x hybrida (pet-tew´-nee-uh)	Petunia	Indirect to low	Moist	**54, 146**
Platycodon grandiflorus (plat-ik-koh´-don)	Balloon flower	Indirect to low	Fresh water	**22**
Rosa (roh´-zuh)	Rose	Indirect to low	Fresh water	**25**
Rudbeckia hirta (rud-bek´-ee-uh)	Black-eyed Susan, 'Gloriosa Daisy'	Indirect to low	Fresh water	**46, 69, 128, 147**
Sedum spectabile (seed´-um)		Indirect to low	Fresh water	**9**
Tagetes erecta (taj-jeet´-eez)	African marigold	Indirect to low	Fresh water	**26, 37, 69**
Verbena (ver-bee´-nuh)		Indirect to low	Moist	**102**
Zinnia (zinn´-ee-uh)		Indirect to low	Fresh water	**53, 69, 100, 147**